EXPLOSIVE BUSINESS

A step-by-step and realistic business guide
to implementing the International Standard: ISO 9001

Steven Burgess

Published by:

Mr. S Burgess

33 Marford Hill

Marford

Wrexham

LL12 8SW

Wales, UK.

ISBN: 978-0-9568056-0-7

Price:£17.97

Foreword

Do you want your business to be recognised, organised, dynamic, modern and forward-looking? Do you want to hit ambitious goals and win the acknowledgement of your peers? Do you want to motivate and empower your workforce?

Then this book is for you.

Obviously, if you're running a business you want it to be successful. But why are some companies so far ahead of the game, while others struggle even to survive?

In my opinion, a lot of this comes down to choice. That might seem surprising; after all, no one would choose to make a business uncompetitive or unsuccessful. Nevertheless, the decisions we take can have a big impact on these areas.

Implementing standards is a case in point. You can choose to put standards in place at your company: or you can choose to ignore them.

Many business owners opt for the latter course, because implementing standards can seem like hard work. But it's always worth bearing in mind the adage "no pain no gain". It's also true that, in this case, the gain can hugely outweigh any pain.

National and international standards are some of the driving forces behind economies. Many vibrant and successful companies are also the ones with such standards in place. Even the United Nations leans upon these pillars to aid businesses, industries and economies.

This book looks at the benefits that implementing a national standard can give to your business. If you have a thirst for improvement, an ambition to succeed and a desire to grow, implementing a standard could turn those dreams into reality. It really could turbo-charge your business – and leave your competitors standing.

About the author

Born and raised in Newcastle under Lyme, Staffordshire, England, Steven Burgess grew up enjoying cricket and football. From his early days he had his eye set on joining the Royal Air Force.

On joining the RAF, Steven quickly became accustomed to managing systems, the engineering excellence demanded of the RAF, legislation and local instruction, standards plans and strategies. Through his own endeavour, teamwork and eventually, overseeing the work of others, he gained expert knowledge of management systems and management structure through the fields of bomb disposal and weapons engineering. He also supervised and helped to manage the tight constraints and requirements of the Explosives Acts and Regulations.

Steven left the Royal Air Force to assist an international petrochemical business with its management systems. He then went on to found his own limited company, Bqmc, alongside isostandardsconsultants.com. This company provides support and helps businesses implement international standards to third party accreditation worldwide.

An engineer by trade, apprenticeship and by university education, Steven now focuses his efforts on precise systems management in occupational health and safety, environmentalism, quality and information security.

His company oversees and guides businesses to put in place precise and bespoke management systems to national accrediting standards. His proactive, straightforward and responsive approach has materially assisted companies to progress their businesses with their clients, local authorities and governments, helping them to achieve high-standing accreditations worldwide.

Acknowledgements

I would like to thank my professional copywriter, Mr. David Vickery for overseeing the book and casting a professional eye over my writing. Also for understanding my thoughts from 300 miles away!

(http://www.dvickery.co.uk/)

Thank you to Bill Slocombe for providing me with auditing opportunities and for being a great ambassador in the world of certification, your certification body is without doubt, one of the most professional auditing / certification bodies in the world and I wish you all the success that you deserve.

If anyone is considering certification to any ISO standard, WCS are truly customer focused and genuinely professional. You cannot go wrong by speaking to them.

http://www.world-cert.co.uk/

Thank you to John Warrington for helping me to try to find a publisher and for being an amazing mentor in business and in life (and on the golf course). You are a great, great man.

(http://www.personalexcellenceinlife.com)

Thank you to Alan Jones, for providing me with the opportunity when I left the Royal Air Force and for giving me a chance to shine. Thank you for trusting me to assist your companies and for being an excellent role model in business. Thank you to you and your Son, Paul, for the opportunities and understanding when I moved on.

(http://www.atsite.co.uk/)

Thanks to Matt Mortimer and James Rae of Mortimer design, for being fantastic, first class programmers, designers of my book cover, websites and other material.

(http://www.mortimerdesign.co.uk/)

Thank you to Paul Plumridge and Peter Bennett for helping me to become a better consultant.

Love to Mum and Dad for being there for us always.

I would like to thank Mel for giving me plenty of support and time to myself during the 11 / 12 months that it has taken me to write this book. I would get in from work, spend time with my family and then back to work again! Thank you so much. Thank you to my daughter Sasha for understanding when I had to work. I love you both.

This book is dedicated to Mel and Sasha, you are wonderful and I love you exponentially more, each day that comes…

Intentionally blank.

This book is dedicated to my family.

Contents

Part 1: Introduction

Part 2: Standards implementation and management

Part 3: Certification and accreditation

Part 4: External professional assistance

The term 'the standard' in this book relates to ISO 9001.

Part 1: Introduction

1.   Standards: vital for better business?

We come across standards in all areas of life. A standard is simply something we are measured against: either by ourselves, or by others.

In business, standards are performance indicators. Having such indicators is vital if we are to measure progress and move ahead. But a process needs to be defined before it can be measured against a standard.

Let me give an example. If I take a ruler and measure a cut piece of string, I am measuring it against a known value or requirement. If the string needs to be six centimetres and is actually five centimetres, clearly it is short by one centimetre. So I can now cut a new piece to the right length.

If you measure a business against a standard and it falls short, you can make changes that will help you improve it. These might involve work by an impartial and accredited third party.

Standards come in many guises. Industry and business use a vast array of standards, some of which are specific to particular sectors or needs. For instance, ISO 14001 (Environmental Management) and BS OHSAS 18001(Occupational Health and Safety Management) are standards that help a business regulate its internal affairs. A standard is not a law, but a method of helping you comply with laws and other regulations.

In this book I will be looking at ISO 9001, one of the best-known standards in the world.

ISO 9001 is a Quality Management Standard that is an important business tool, practised worldwide. It has been consistently improved over the past few decades and can certainly help you develop your business – provided it is used properly.

10

Some people think of standards as dull and uninteresting. Nothing could be further from the truth. They are actually weapons for your business, helping it to succeed, prosper and out-manoeuvre its rivals.

The outside world, and in particular existing and potential customers, may view you far more favourably if you have implemented a recognised standard. This is especially so if they are comparing two prospective suppliers, one which is accredited to a relevant standard and one which is not.

The reasons are not hard to find. The standard announces that your business is proactive, caring, responsible, progressive. Action is good.

Many factors can drive that action. The most common ones are "Our customer wants us to have it", "We can't get onto the tender list without it", "We see it as an effective part of our marketing strategy" and "We want it to help us to drive the business forward, to control our methods and have an objective standard which we can measure ourselves against". But it doesn't matter. Even if you're impelled by just one driver, you can still reap benefits in a wide range of areas – right across your operations, in fact.

While the first three drivers mentioned above are guided by external forces – in these cases, customers, local authorities and marketing the business – the last one is something that the business itself is choosing to do, to help it develop professionally. That's all about being responsible, proactive and forward-thinking.

Suppose you were a customer and had two suppliers. Supplier A had already implemented ISO 9001 on its own initiative. You now have to inform the people at Supplier B that you need them to do the same. Which one are you likely to be more impressed by? And given those attitudes, which one will you source more supplies from, other things being equal?

The next question must be, why do companies choose not to implement standards such as ISO 9001? There are the knee-jerk reactions such as "I can't be bothered with that, it takes too long, the paperwork is unnecessary, the auditors know nothing about our work," and so on. There are more valid reasons such as lacking the funds and other resources to put a standard in place. Whatever the reason, though, not implementing a standard can be detrimental to your company's health. Increasingly, people want to do business with companies perceived as serious, responsible and effective: and having ISO 9001 proclaims those qualities to the world.

ISO standards are entirely voluntary and ISO is a non-governmental organisation. ISO does not have the authority to enforce its standards; but some companies may elect to adopt them, particularly those concerned with the environment, health and safety or security. They may also be referred to in legislation and regulation because they provide the technical basis or standard which has been agreed and set by worldwide deliberation and acceptance.

In the case of ISO 9001, it is sometimes viewed as an effective marketing tool. I would agree with those who see it that way – but I would go a lot further. Even if you adopt it largely for that reason, you will find that it can transform the effectiveness of your operations across the board. Not surprisingly, it is prominently displayed by many a successful business.

ISO 9001, once implemented, impinges on all areas of an organisation, producing improvements and enhancements to procedures and working methods. It has been called "the worker that is never seen," because it's like having an invisible but very effective extra team on your payroll!

When a standard is part of the fabric of your business, it really can make a difference to your success. If you are prepared, any standard will help you. But do people and businesses want to be helped? That's the question. For those that do and choose a standard to assist them, they have something to measure their effectiveness against. It's a vital aid to success and greater profitability. Best of all, it's not just a one-off gain but an ongoing improvement to your operations.

Standards make such an important contribution to our lives and are overwhelmingly positive. The supreme dedication in the armed forces, for instance, comes from professionalism, dedication, actions – and standards. Without standards, discipline and professionalism would be nothing. They are the flag-bearers of excellence and fortitude. If you want discipline and professionalism in your business, standards can help you achieve them.

If you've read this far, the chances are that those qualities are exactly what you want in your business. So let's go on to explore what implementing a standard means.

2.   ISO: What's in a name?

ISO (or the International Organization for Standardization as it is less commonly known) is the world's largest developer and publisher of International Standards.

Delegates from 25 countries met in London in 1946 and decided to create a new international organisation. Its objective was to "facilitate the international coordination and unification of industrial standards".

The new organisation, called ISO, officially began life on 23 February 1947. Based in Geneva, ISO is financed by its national members, whose subscriptions help to meet the cost of the administrative division of ISO, the Central Secretariat. Another source of income is generated by selling standards. And, if you haven't found out already, they can be quite costly.

Some institutions ask you to become a member (at a price) and charge you far less for buying the standards. Depending on what you buy, this could be well worth your while; or it could put you out of pocket. Check which ones you need and work out the cost differences.

ISO also collaborates with its partners in international standardisation, IEC (the International Electro-technical Commission) and ITU (the International Telecommunication Union). The three organisations are based in Geneva and have formed the World Standards Cooperation (WSC) to act as a focal point for partnership and promotion of international standardisation.

The World Trade Organisation (WTO) is immensely appreciative of the way in which standardisation breaks down international barriers to trade. ISO also collaborates with the United Nations and helps to regulate and harmonise policy, rules and requirements. One of the organisations that ISO supports is the World Health Organisation (WHO). ISO, in short, is massive and far-reaching.

ISO also provides backing and support to developing countries. What has worked internationally and nationally will certainly help developing nations to progress.

I like to call ISO the United Nations of business. I don't think that's too fanciful; when you delve into what it does and what it stands for, it brings businesses and countries together to form common standards, values, platforms and bonds. Much like the United Nations but with considerably fewer conflicts!

ISO is a network of national standards organisations which to date reaches 159 countries. It brings these nations and organisations together and combines it all with a Central Secretariat in Geneva which coordinates the system very effectively.

ISO builds bridges between sectors in different countries. Some of the organisations within it are sponsored and attached to government, whereas others are brought together by private companies and national partnerships willing to combine efforts in reaching common standards and policy. Therefore, ISO enables a consensus to be reached on solutions that meet both the requirements of business and the broader needs of society.

What's in a name?

The International Organization for Standardization derives its name from the Greek word "isos", which means equal.

The founders of the organisation chose this meaning because it was important that the term should be used and understood universally. If they had simply translated the phrase into other languages, there would have been no such universal recognition; it would have been IOS in English, OIN in French (Organisation internationale de normalisation), and so on. With "isos" meaning equal, the choice was a natural one, and the result is that ISO is the format in every language. It's also short, memorable and catchy, which always helps.

International standards now number over 17000 and rising: an impressive achievement in a relatively short time. Their programmes span a wide range of businesses and sectors, encompassing engineering, agriculture, construction, transport, distribution, environmental, medical devices, information technology, food, communication, management practice and services.

Standards help maintain the desirable characteristics of products and services such as quality control, environmental management, safety, reliability, efficiency and interchangeability.

It's a funny thing, though. When products and services meet our expectations, we tend to underestimate the role the standard may have played in delivering that result. It is taken for granted because most of the time standards are unseen, apart from when you notice them on a company's reception wall or on the back of an electricity plug, and even then they are easily overlooked. However, standards tend to be become conspicuous by their absence. Products or services can become unreliable, incompatible, and possibly even dangerous?

This is why standards are so important in our everyday life. What if our trains or buses had no standards? What if the airlines didn't bother with them? Imagine coming on board your airliner and seeing the door to the cockpit swinging open, inviting passengers to wander in and distract the crew. What if they operated the controls in a disorganised and careless manner? What if the cabin crew didn't care about you wearing your seatbelt or telling you about emergency procedures? You would probably worry all the way to your destination.

An extreme example, perhaps: but the fact remains that, without standards, the world would be a chaotic and dangerous place. If we had no standards in bomb disposal and weapons engineering, I probably would not have been around to write this book.

Fortunately, ISO oversees the process of many standards and helps businesses to progress while aiding them to be better at what they do. This makes them more professional, helps them take greater pride in their work and offer a better service. One day, that service may even be unrivalled as a result. This may not be the case for all companies, as many are professional and competent without standards, they may have their own internal standards that are far more important and necessary. The ISO systems and standards will complement these.

The next time you shun a standard by saying, "ISO is too hard" or "That's not for us, we don't need it," think again. What if your car, bus or train didn't have standards? What if the people who drove around you were not licensed and the Driving Standards Agency did not exist?

Standards are vital for setting the baseline of what is acceptable. But that's just the start. Standards in business can sweep through your organisation like a benevolent virus to give you more rigorous and robust processes, a far more organised and profitable business – all leading to a compelling competitive edge.

Suddenly, standards don't sound either boring or irrelevant.

3.   How are standards incorporated and formulated?

As I mentioned in the last chapter, there are now over 17,000 international standards in place. This means that new standards are frequently being introduced. So what is the procedure for this?

ISO oversees the process. It will launch and develop new standards in response to demand from sectors that establish a requirement for them and which will benefit from their implementation.

This works as follows. A sector or organisation will contact one of the national ISO bodies or the ISO itself and communicate that it needs a standard. There may then be the need to propose the new item to a technical committee responsible for overseeing the implementation of standards in a particular field or sector.

Sometimes a particular sector may not be covered; and in this case, proposals can be made to formulate new technical committees to cover new fields of activity. Professionals in that field will need to form the backbone of any new technical committee.

For a standard to be accepted for development, it must receive the majority support of the participating members of the technical committee in which it is involved. It must also have global relevance. A group of people cannot simply get together and demand a standard; it must be desired nationally or internationally.

Who develops ISO standards?

International Standards (ISO Standards) are developed by the technical committees of the fields that they represent. These will comprise experts from the technical, business, industrial and information technology sectors which have requested standards. The experts will be joined by government representatives, agencies, testing laboratories, consumer groups, associations, third parties and academic professionals interested in developing standards for their sector.

If a new technical committee is required, proposals to develop it are submitted to all of the ISO Member bodies. If these are approved, the chair is formally appointed by the Technical Management Board. To get the green light you basically need acceptance from the members and the technical management board as well as the Secretariat, which is the body providing administrative support to the work of the committee.

The ISO rules state that the national member body must take into account views of all parties interested in a standard under development. This then allows them to present their case with greater consolidation and effect when proposals are to be made and presented.

Interestingly, private international, regional and local organisations and the public sector may apply for a liaison status that allows them to be deeply involved in the development of a standard. These organisations have no voting rights but can propose modifications to drafts or new items. They can even ask for a "fast tracking" of a standard, which means a standard has already been developed but requires authority and acceptance.

So the world of standards is far more involved than many would suspect. The involvement and cooperation is both global and deeply embedded to a level rarely encountered elsewhere.

Now you are getting a flavour of ISO Standards, the depth of their organisation and the myriad opportunities they may present to you and your company. Perhaps you can already see the benefits of having your company accepted into what is in effect a worldwide club. These standards are brought to our knowledge by highly skilled and professional organisations and people. I want to be in the same boat as them – and I imagine you do too.

Visit ISO at http://www.iso.org

Perhaps you are worried about the implementation of standards in your business and the effects this may have? Perhaps you would like to implement a standard but are not sure how to approach it or the knowledge to start. If so, seek advice. A standard may just be the kick that your business needs.

Part 2: Standards implementation and management

4.   Quality Management Systems: what do they do?

Quality Management Systems are a set of procedures that help you control your company. These can improve the management and coordination of key business areas.

A Quality Management System, or QMS as it is also known, is a systematic and methodical approach to maintain important and often-overlooked aspects of a business.

When people start businesses, it's usual to focus on the operational and financial necessities such as products or services, income and outgoings, expenditure and delivery. A Quality Management System helps you focus on other important aspects: documentation, safety, testing, qualification, monitoring, purchasing, product quality, management involvement, review of business procedure, necessary corrective actions and customer satisfaction.

I'm often surprised to find that many businesses that use me as a consultant are quite out of touch with both their expenditure *and* their customers. And yet these are the two business factors in determining whether a business flourishes or fails. That's not surprising. If you spend too much and lack discipline with money, your business may go to the wall. If you don't look after your customers, you can lose them *and* your business.

So why do a high percentage of businesses not target these areas? That's a good question. I think some businesses are so focused on what they want and what they are delivering to the customer, they actually forget about what it is that brought them the custom in the first place. Sometimes greed or cost-cutting gets in the way.

Custom drives our products and services, and demand brings custom – so why not focus on keeping customers satisfied and meeting their after-sales requirements? This is why ISO 9001 helps. Business is about the customer, not what cars the directors drive.

Let's look at expenditure. Many businesses fail to control their expenditure well. They have no forecasting systems, no proper budgeting. I once met someone who had a company for many years. When I asked them what the purchasing procedure was and who controlled it, I was told that nobody did; the staff just asked if it was all right to buy something, and the answer was usually yes! Where is the control or business logic there? This person was lovely, but they didn't know what their company was spending. How could they manage what went out of the door if they were not sure what came in?

ISO 9001 can help here, as in many other areas. It doesn't necessarily look at what you spend but it does demand that you put in place a procedure to control purchasing, written or otherwise. The point is that purchasing is an extremely important part of business, so why not control it?

A QMS is designed to help you in business. If you don't need help in this area, I assume you're a millionaire who is reading this book for fun. For the rest of us, this book is about dedicated assistance and the importance of implementing a structured business system audited by an accurate and responsible accrediting / certificating body.

A Quality Management System is an approach that is measured. You can see the changes, you can see your objectives and goals, you can see what's going right and what's going wrong. These are valuable aids: and the more the QMS is involved in your business, the greater chance of success.

A QMS also helps to galvanise your team and staff. Why? Because systems give people an idea of where they are going and what to do if they are at a loss. How will your staff know where they are going – and for that matter, where the business is going, if they don't know the direction or the correct procedures? Businesses in this condition are standing still. And as we all know, businesses that stop moving very quickly start to go backwards.

Human beings want structure; take that away and the consequences can be dire. So dire in fact that they may even forget what to do when they are at work. You may laugh at this idea, but I have seen it happen. Please don't blame your staff if you are a business owner, director or manager who lacks direction. If you don't have direction, there is a good chance that your staff won't either. They are also likely to think you quite unprofessional, or maybe even an idiot?

It's really quite simple. If staff realise that neither the business nor its managers know where they're going and are slack with their control, they will flow out of the company like an outgoing tide. Even some who remain may be lacklustre and underperforming. Does that ring alarm bells or sound familiar to you? ISO 9001 can help you with the structure of your business and turn your losses around – if you apply it with effort and dedication.

One pertinent area in any company is training. I always impress on companies that spending on training is not a drain on their resources but a profitable investment.

Why? Because you are adding staff and company value all of the time, there is no negative to training. If you educate staff, they are far more likely to feel involved, happy that you care about them and pleased that you are helping them in life's advancement. This is one of the most important parts of business.

Nevertheless, in four out of five companies I talk to, the conversation goes like this.

Me: What education and training do your people require?

Senior Manager: Er, well… we just tell them what to do really.

Me: Do you have you a job description and a list of educational requirements?

SM: Oh no, we don't feel we need those.

Me: Well, maybe it's time you put them in place.

SM: But how much will it cost?

As I suggested earlier, it's not about how much it costs but about the return you get on your investment. A training programme that raised your staff productivity and morale 200 per cent would certainly be worth the money it took.

A Quality Management System ensures that your staff are well trained. If they are not, the auditors will pick up on it and inform you that you need to take action; and eventually your certificate may be revoked if you do not carry out training or provide effective resources.

To summarise, expenditure, customer service and training are three of some of the top priorities for any business.

Quality Management Systems are a controlling point. One or two, or maybe even more people will control them, depending on the structure, size and the complexity of a business.

A system is there to remove excuses, concentrate on improvement and try to push your business boundaries to encourage professionalism…and eventually, boost profit.

The facts bear out my view: systems help make us safer, cleaner and more efficient – and yes, more profitable.

A Quality Management System also looks at your policies, company objectives, management structure and framework for reporting. It looks at your customers' needs and your own requirements: can you deliver what you have promised?

Self assessment and improvement is a tried and tested method of raising self-awareness and finding logical answers to your problems. If you know what is wrong, you can fix it: if you don't, you can't. Stick your head in the sand and your problems will only mount up grow. Face them head on and watch them gradually fade away – with time and effort.

Embrace a quality management standard and it will help you and your business.

5.   Effective ISO Management

My definition of "effective" is quite simple: it is something that works. While it's possible to stumble upon effectiveness, it's more usually the result of careful planning.

It's not hard to see that such planning can often pay dividends. In business, for instance, more effective processes or services can make you more efficient – and more profitable.

Effective ISO Management is underpinned by an attribute often lacking in businesses regardless of standards or not; and that is action. Get it done, don't make excuses, and don't blame others for lack of progress. Doing and acting are the fundamentals of good business practice, excuses and procrastinating can be burdensome in many cases.

In my experience, 95 per cent of problems facing an organisation, may be due to inaction, poor management, overspending, not controlling your budget, buying expensive cars and business premises when there is no need, and so on. In such circumstances, it's idle to try and shift the blame to others, or to bad luck. (I've found that the people who work the hardest are also the "luckiest".) Luck in my eyes is where action and getting things done meets a possible opportunity, putting yourself in the right place will increase your fortunes and will naturally occur just by way of action.

In other words, if you want to get something done and move forward, stop blaming other factors and become efficient. Most companies go bust because they either spend too much or borrow too much. Efficiency is paramount and a standard helps you to become more efficient.

If you want something done in life, you have to do it yourself; and the best way to implement a management system of any kind is through action and encouragement.

People who get on with their lives impress me. Of course, trying to achieve something means leaving your comfort zone and challenging yourself. But that's the only way to be effective. You have to leave your comfort zone, and in business, that may mean embracing a standard?

If you want the personification of effectiveness, look at Lord Alan Sugar, Sir Richard Branson, Simon Cowell and others like them. There's no doubt that they "do action and effectiveness". Naturally, they have their critics – as does anyone in the public eye. But they wouldn't ever have been in the public eye unless they had been highly effective at what they do.

Take Branson, for instance. He was dyslexic and had poor academic performance, leaving school at 16. He could have sat around bemoaning his "bad luck" – but instead he took action. He published a magazine called "Student" that same year of leaving school. Four years later he started an audio record mail-order business. Today, there are over 360 companies in the Virgin brand, and he is one of the 300 richest people on the planet. An amazing man.

Simon Cowell had a fiver in his pocket to get him home to his Mum's when he went bust, now he is one of the richest men on the planet, he could have sat around moaning, I'm sure he did a little bit and maybe he was entitled to do so? That said, he picked himself up and now drives a Rolls Royce, that is the personification of get up and go. Well done to him. Duncan Bannatyne started with an Ice Cream van, then built some nursing homes and look at him now, great people get on with their work. Alan Sugar is now a Lord and is the UK's most recognisable businessman alongside Sir Richard, Lord Sugar started by putting computer parts together, now he has millions, why? Getting things done and being efficient. You may have heard him saying that he doesn't like "Steady Eddies" or "Smoozers", whatever they are, they are not people who are effective. Effective at talking rubbish I suspect.

You might say that the world is divided into two classes of people: those who are effective, and those who are not. People in the latter group spend lots of time sitting around in coffee bars and pubs, talking about the effective ones: mocking them, yes, but also envying them. I have no doubt which group I'd rather be in! But to take action, to make progress, we need to be effective.

Effectiveness doesn't just need action, it *is* action. It is encouragement and self-worth. Self-belief is a vital tool of the trade. It will help you to implement standards.

So, let me give you a list of ideas that will help you in your quest for improvement. I will start in the same way I begin all of my projects and consultancy, which is to take a step back and look at the company.

Firstly, what are the **goals of the company and where do you want the company to go?** What is the director's vision and **what is the reason for implementing a system of worth?** This is important. When I go into a company, before the consultancy project starts, I always ask: **what do you want out of the system and what do you want out of me?**

I like to ask these questions to establish a baseline. The answers tell me what level of assistance the directors need – and also let me accurately predict how serious they are. I can then gauge how best to help them.

Most companies seeking to implement a management system do so for one of three reasons:

1) For marketing purposes.

2) Because customers want the company to have it.

3) To make progress and help with structure.

These reasons make a big difference to their approach. Let me explain. If a company wants me to go in and complete their standards for marketing purposes, they usually want me not to be seen, not to bother anybody and come in with the minimum of fuss, time and cost. They drag their feet when making a decision, cannot do much for themselves and want me to take the whole workload on in about eight days. In effect, they just want the certificate on the wall.

I obviously do what they ask for; but it saddens me, because I know I could do a lot more for them in terms of helping them become more effective. With this in mind, if your company is in the same mind-set, my advice is to start slowly. As you increase momentum you build friends and accomplices that are on board with your plans. It takes time to build relationships and people feel awkward about new projects, especially if it brings more work to their desks. Don't worry! Take a deep breath and introduce new methods slowly. If you get at least one director on your side, that can be half the battle won.

I once implemented a system for a business. One of its employees was a thorn in my side. All I wanted him to do was complete one form for ISO 9001. This form had seven sections to complete: five of the sections were name, date, project reference, person spoken to and signature, and the remaining two were comments and possible corrective actions. One line had to be completed per week, which took about 30 seconds. Sounds simple, but hell would have frozen over before he complied. I'd only known him for about two months when I asked him to do it and he was wary of this project (and me). Sometimes you just have to do it yourself, so I did.

Effectiveness is all about the implementer. If colleagues won't help you, do it yourself, even if it means making a mistake.

In the case of that gentleman, he became a good friend in time and did most of what I asked of him – once he trusted me. Effectiveness is about breaking through barriers, it is about people relationships. ISO effectiveness is about breaking barriers with people from other departments and showing them that you are there to **help, not hinder**.

Some companies phone me up and say, can we have a certificate and then can you complete the work? I say no, every time. Some might scoff at me for turning away income. But I don't do certificates; I work impartially from certification bodies and help companies gain the highest levels of accreditation. Secondly, I do not work for people who cut corners because this suggests that they might also cut corners with their safety, ethics or quality (not to mention their readiness to pay their consultants).

It's also impossible to help those that are convinced they do not need the assistance or the standard; and if one or more directors are like this, you are in for a rough ride. I had one company approach me and tell me that a major and substantial customer of theirs wanted them to have a certain system in place. They also told me that the customer threatened to pull the plug on them for a massive contract. One of the directors said to me, "I'm not convinced about implementing this?"

This system would have cost a few thousand pounds at most. Set that against the prospect of alienating a key client, losing a mega-contract and possibly downsizing operations and there would seem to be nothing to think about. But he wasn't convinced.

In the end, as I said previously, it was all about barriers. I completed their system and the person I worked alongside was admirably effective in everything I asked him to do. It remains one of the best management systems I have seen to this day.

Then there is the type of company that really wants assistance. The directors invite me in formally, they thank me for coming, they are polite and courteous. From the first meetings, they sit forward and listen to me. These companies want action and they are prepared to try new things and push on. They are the ones that are going to be successful. They value objective opinion and are thirsty for advancement. They pay you so fast you've hardly had time to get home and have your dinner.

I love these companies and I love helping them. Not because of quick payment but because of their desire to improve. I enjoy examining the progression and trying new methods and procedures with them. There is plenty of dialogue and interaction. We complement each other and we move the company forward in this modern world of change.

Proactive companies are adapters, changers and the optimisers. If something isn't working, they change it or change their conditions accordingly. If you work for a company that is proactive, you're half-way there.

So what are the next stages of effective approach?

Firstly I would establish a **common electronic file from which to write, review, amend and distribute documents** to the whole company. Too many companies have different documents floating about. You need control. Some may say I am a control freak; I don't agree, but I am in favour of structure. With structure comes progression, ease of management and further effectiveness.

I'll look at documentation in further detail when we discuss "4.2.3" control of documents later in this section, but for now you need to control it.

One more thing: if your company is big and the documentation is spread out, then get people involved in each department, tell them what you are doing, get their bosses on board and get them to control the documents in their section. Just tell them that if they don't, it could cause problems when the audit comes. People, once on board, will not want to let you down; so use this to your advantage – in a scrupulous way.

If people won't come on board, try another way. On audit, I once gave a company a non conformity for consistent abuse of the disabled parking bay slots (this wasn't a Quality Management System). One able-bodied manager took it upon himself to park there because he felt like it. I warned them that I was going to give them a non conformity it if he kept breaking the law.

An overreaction on my part? I don't think so. Why should people deprive a disabled person just because they cannot bother to walk an extra 10 metres? What if the UKAS auditor was disabled? What if a customer was disabled or a person was in need? The health and safety manager at that company gave him a ticking off. Serves him right, you tend to find that people let management systems down rather than the actual system itself.

This story proves that you cannot control everything, so stick to what you can control and ask politely. In the case of the documentation side, just explain the reason why you are trying to control it, put the seed into their heads, keep on at them now and again and ask for help if you need it. Move on and go back to it.

The next step for effective approach is the **written aspect** of any system. **Firstly purchase the standards** from the ISO Store, TSO Bookshop or from the BSI Shop. The standards usually come with an effective guidance document too. After you have purchased the standard(s), you need to **familiarise yourself with them.**

It pays to shop around for standards and it is usually a good idea to get someone to help you who has been involved with this before – provided that is really the case. Many people say that they have past experience when they have merely been audited in the past for a few minutes or have completed a few documents for ISO projects here and there. Make sure anyone you get help from really has effectively implemented a management system or had detailed involvement as a second party.

Beware though, many a person have I come across that says "I've done this before." What is their interpretation of "done this before"? It usually means that they may have been audited in the past (for a few minutes) or they had to fill in a few documents for ISO projects here and there.

"Done this before" in my head is interpreted by effectively implementing a management system, or having detailed involvement as a second party, not filling in a few documents here and there! The two principles are a "pacific" apart. Find out what they mean if someone says "I've done this before".

The next stage is one of the most important parts to get going. **Look at each part of the standard** from section 4.0 onwards until you reach 8.5.3, at the end. Please read all of the other sections (1, 2 and 3 + annexes) and keep them in mind but remember that you are audited on the requirements in between sections **4.0 and 8.5.3**. (This may change slightly in the future when amendments are made.)

Look at each part of the standard, include subdivisions e.g. 4.1, 4.2.1, 4.2.2 etc. You need to find out what each part of the standard means to you and your business. Although the standard does not tell you what to do in your business, it tells you what is required to comply with assessment. Please read it properly.

The effectiveness of implementation hangs on interpreting the standard into your company. This is what I specialise in.

I always look at the company and decide where I can fit the business into the descriptions and subdivisions. When I have completed that part I then look at what the company is missing and make suggestions to comply. We then take these suggestions forward and decide on the most effective course of action for that company.

To clarify, take 4.2 Documentation Requirements and 4.2.1 General. It tells you that you need a quality manual, documented statements of a quality policy, and quality objectives.

For this, your company will need to write a manual. As I have explained, write each of the standard subdivisions down and decide where your company fits into these categories. Section 5 of this chapter will help you to identify what to do, how to implement it into your business and decide what every division and subdivision means for you and your company.

The next step is to fulfil the documentation requirements. As you go through this book I will tell you what is required, and point out mandatory items that you should not miss. Sometimes I will also tell you what is mandatory for me, but not mandatory in the standard. From experience I know what helps and will be of benefit to you.

Written procedures are one of those requirements that you cannot dodge. There are six of them in ISO 9001:2008: Control of Documents, Control of Records, Control of Non conforming Product, Internal Audit, Corrective action and Preventive action.

You need to establish a written procedure for these six, using the above headings or similar. The standard will tell you at each of these sections that a documented procedure should be present. So you'll need to write one that is applicable to your company. If you write them at the start and find out how the company may already control its non conforming products or audits, then please go and speak to people.

Ask them how they are doing. Say to them, "I would like to help to improve your system." No one objects to having their work made easier and more effective. Pay attention to what people say, offer sincere and genuine help, and they will cooperate.

To summarise, you have enlisted support, you have obtained a copy of the standard and are reviewing it, your documentation planning is in order, and you are aware of how to control the documentation you already use.

The next part is to build the momentum – a highly effective process. Now that you have people who have bought into your plans, it is time to flow the requirements into the framework of your business.

6.   Starting considerations

So you can see the benefits of ISO implementation. But what aspects should you consider before going ahead with it?

The most important consideration is whether your company can cope with the extra demand that implementation may place on some staff. You must ensure that your staff can already cope with their workload, and that you're not adding to an already heavy burden so that they end up taking time off work due to stress. After all, ISO 9001 is designed to make your business better, not hurt it! Once properly implemented, the maintenance may be minimal and should never be burdensome to current practises. It will be wise to keep your audits and management reviews up to date each year.

When implementing, it is about finding the gaps in your organisation that the standard demands are in place. You do not usually need a brand new system of work, unless you really need to. Implementing standards is about bolstering and improving your current processes, never lose sight of that, the organisation is not usually about to dramatically change just to suit a standard.

It's not always easy to select the best person when starting this task. Let me explain. If yours is an engineering company, then the last person you should choose is someone who knows little about engineering. It would be wise not to choose the accountant, or the purchaser, or the storeman (with all due respect). It should be someone who knows engineering relatively well: or at least someone who knows the company relatively well. But, I hear you say, that could be the accountant or the buyer or the storeman! True; but what I am referring to is knowledge of a subject that is important in a particular company.

An engineering company will probably opt for an engineer or similar because he knows the engineering systems, he knows what controls may be in place, be familiar with design matters (highly important if your company designs its products), he will know specifications, understand testing procedures and be able to tie processes together. If he can do most of that and has a good grasp of quality, an engineer or technician would be the ideal choice in that environment.

In a manufacturing company the situation is somewhat different. You could choose an accomplished supervisor, manufacturing manager or a shop floor manager, someone who knows the processes and has a degree of responsibility already. That goes for any sector.

Or, choose someone with a bit of flair, some get up and go in them, even if they don't know the business that well.

This may sound like I'm contradicting myself. But sometimes you may be forced to choose an inexperienced company member due to other factors. If so, make sure it is someone who acts with conviction, has plenty of vision and drive. A "wet lettuce" who can be trodden on will never implement ISO properly.

Implementation needs to be given to someone with backbone and integrity: and definitely not a "yes man". Such people may tell you what you want to hear, but they won't get you the desired results of action and open dialogue.

If possible, I'd recommend you give the role to someone who is both responsible and likeable. This type of person is far more likely to get people to come on board; and they are more likely to be listened to than are people with little or no responsibility.

This is hardly surprising; if you choose an apprentice to do it, no one will listen to him and he probably won't have the experience to deal with it anyway. You need someone who can tell staff to do things as well as ask them (politely). Usually you need a bit of authority for these roles. If a person has just joined and is tasked with implementation, as I explained earlier, people are far less likely to do something for someone that they do not know. Rapport and trust need to be built first. If someone is respected, they have a great head start.

People also need to be able to take a bit of "stick" when making changes, act on their beliefs, bring teams together, and smooth out relationship problems. This may suggest that you'd be better off appointing a marriage counsellor! But in any company, egos can get frayed and tensions arise, especially with something new such as ISO 9001 implementation. At such times, you need someone who can calm people down, soothe any sense of grievance or annoyance, encourage togetherness and act as a go-between.

To summarise, choose someone who gets on with their work, is liked, has an in-depth knowledge of the company and a good level of responsibility.

Consultants

Later on in this book, I will look at what a consultant does and what they can help you with. But at this stage, let me just make these points. If you are going to get someone to help you, ask them to come and see you or telephone them. Find out if they have experience in your field and of implementing ISO projects. Ask them if they are an ISO 9001 auditor for example and do they do any work for a company that provides auditing services?

Don't worry unduly if they haven't too much experience in your sector; try and see what that person can bring to your business. I know some great consultants and auditors who are engineers. If they were asked to go into a care home to put an ISO 9001 system into there, I can imagine them doing a fantastic job. Please keep your options open and don't exclude a consultant on the grounds of lacking specific industry experience.

Beware, ask the consultant or company what their credentials are, and find out whether they have any certificates or evidence of experience in these subjects. Ask them if they do any third party audits for UKAS or ANAB or another ISO body. Because they'll tell you what to expect on audit, this is valuable expertise that you can benefit from.

Of course, it doesn't apply to all. There are some excellent consultancies out there that do not have the auditor qualifications or lots of experience in implementing these standards. In this type of case, dig deeper: find out who they have worked for and ask to speak to those companies.

Get a sample of at least two or three companies for quotes and go from there. The best route in my opinion is to use someone who has the auditor qualifications and is also an auditor in his/her spare time for National Certification bodies, such as WCS, BSI, NQA and Moody International, there are others too, check out he internet for further information, I'll also discuss certification bodies later in this book.

Also, ask whether the company offering you consultancy has an ISO 9001 Management System and certificate of their own. In other words, do they practise what they preach? And if they don't have one in place, why not? I can hear the excuses from here to Australia.

Have they themselves been third-party audited by a UKAS/ANAB accredited body? If they are so good at helping others, why are they not audited themselves to ensure that they are doing the right job for you? What have they to hide if they do not have a certificate to ISO 9001 that is third-party accredited? Or any other standard for that matter.

If you are really worried about who to choose, check out ISO 10019 which is an international standard for choosing a quality management consultant. There are standards for everything!

These are reasonable questions to put to a company. Bear in mind, though, that a consultant operating on his own will probably not have a standard for their business. If this is so, ask about experience and qualifications.

Get the right person and company for you. Also, there are some people who consult and write their own certificates; some businesses and organisations such as the Ministry of Defence or the Government may only accept third-party accredited standards, whatever you choose, it must be right for you.

My company, bqmc co uk limited, is ISO 9001 and ISO 14001 accredited with a UKAS accredited body. My priorities are in making sure that my company does the best for our customers and that we are environmentally friendly in the process. So ISO 9001 works for me. The certification body makes sure that my company is completing the correct ISO implementation work with our clients; my quality management system is a back-up for our customers. (If you want to check, my company is registered with World Certification Services in Liverpool, UK.)

Appearances are often a pointer. If the consultant that is after your money is scruffy, unkempt, unprofessional looking, they may be equally untidy with your management system. But as I say, standards start with your own; invest wisely. We'll discuss this in greater detail later.

What else needs to be considered at the start?

Let's assume you now have the green light, you've chosen the person to head the task has and he or she has the backing of the board. The next step is that training **must** be considered.

If you want to complete the project yourself without outside help, then it would be very wise to do a training course. There are many providers of training courses and I can help you choose the best one for you. When you are audited, the auditor may want to see your training record. Relevant qualifications will be well perceived. The qualification will also ensure that you will get more things right on audit.

Ask yourself what you want to get out of your training. Is it awareness in the subject? Is it internal auditing training as well so that you can complete your internal audits? Is it an auditor qualification (a five-day course) to gain the highest auditing award? You will have to weigh up your options. Choose what you need to do, and discuss this with a certification body and your boss.

Excellent providers of training are BQMC, WCS, BSI, ISOQAR, Moody International and JPD. I mention those because I have done courses with all of them. I shall tell you more about them later; but for now, give them a call and ask what courses they do. Check the prices out to suit your budget, ask them for some advice and see which one suits you best. You will almost certainly find something to please you from within this recommended group. Get plenty of information from them, they will be very helpful.

The International Register of Certified Auditors (IRCA) also audit some training bodies to make sure that their training is to a common standard. It is like a third-party assessment, except that they check training instead of a company management system. However, not all companies do this; personally, the course is usually about how good the instructor is and the quality of the course content.

Some courses provided by those I mentioned are IRCA-approved; these are usually the Lead Auditor courses. If you ask the companies concerned they will be able to inform you if their courses are approved. If they are not, just ask what the details are. All the above companies have an excellent reputation and should stand you in good stead.

If it is a small company providing training, just check their credentials out a little further and ask for a few referees – and check that these referees are not friends and family! (Believe me, it happens).

The three courses that you may wish to consider are the following. I have chosen these because they are widely attended, are usually good value for money and are proven to help. I'll just tell you the overview.

Awareness day course - gives you insight into a standard and may last between 1 to 2 days with some companies. This will tell you how to approach a standard and give you some great tips on implementation. Ideas will be flowing freely and you should get a lot out of it as well as hearing about other people's experiences, which is often helpful. The courses can also provide a great forum, so they are worth the money.

Internal auditing courses give you a deeper insight into a standard and prepare you for internal auditing of your company to the ISO 9001 standard. You will enjoy role-playing and lots of teamwork. It is great fun and very precise. It should last around 2-3 days. Before you go into this, if ISO 9001 is new to you, purchase a copy of the standard and make yourself familiar with it before you go on the course.

Reading it thoroughly will pay dividends. It can be hard walking into a training course if you haven't even looked at a standard. Do yourself a favour and read ISO 9001 properly before attending. Even if it is just a few hours of work time, use it well and you will be pleased that you did.

Auditor/Lead Auditor courses can last for up to 5 days. These give a full insight into the standard and are very in depth. This type of course prepares you for the rigours of internal and external 2nd / 3rd party audits. It prepares you for auditing on behalf of a certification body too. This course is for the serious auditors and company representatives. When I did mine, I took a week's holiday off from the company that I worked for. It was hard work, but very worthwhile. I knew the standard well at this point and I will say to you that if you choose this option, prepare for hard work and an exam at the end. You will need to know the standard well.

If you want to pass, be ready to put in the hours at home after the course and pass practical and theory tests to get your "successful" certificate.

I was on the course with people who had never even read the standard. Not surprisingly, they struggled! If you choose the five-day course, prepare thoroughly and don't be afraid of hard work; the results will make it worth your while.

There are many other courses available, and many providers, so check out their websites. Good luck with your training.

Another important matter when starting is to team up with an ally. This could be a friend that you get along well with, someone who will sympathise with your problems and may be able to help you in times of need.

A director is often a great ally; someone who commands authority and is liked is a great asset to you, and can often help with funding. I had a gentleman and a Managing Director called Alan, I'll talk more about Alan in section 21. Director buy-in is in the next section, so I will cover more then.

When I did my first ISO 9001 project, my friend Bob helped me at times. He was great. He was a health and safety expert so he knew about standards; and he was also a fine stalwart of the company. This helped me because if I couldn't get leverage, Bob could and he helped me to smooth the process in some areas of the business. I was relatively new and sometimes people didn't listen to me, but Bob was usually able to sort them out!

How large is your company?

If you are in a small company you have an advantage over those people trying to put this system into a larger company.

What do I mean by small and large? Numbers of people and numbers of sites are the main factors. If you work in a company with one site and no more than

twenty-five people, it's much easier than someone trying to do the same thing with multiple sites and a far larger workforce.

The smaller company typically has middle and senior management that are easy to converse with. You can get hold of them, you probably see them almost every day, and if you want something sanctioned, for example financial or training resources, this is usually easier to arrange.

Even in smaller companies, it can be difficult to get a reply from a manager to an email or a request. If you need to ask a manager for some funding or resources, go and ask in person. Keep pestering them (in a friendly and polite way) until you get what you need.

If you work in a large company and this is all new, you definitely have a task on your hands. To start with, you may need a consultant: s/he will help to break it all down for you and provide useful help once they get a grip of your business. Even if you only use them for a day or two, the guidance offered may be invaluable and point you in the best direction instead of wandering off course aimlessly without knowing.

When larger companies put these standards in, there are more barriers to overcome, more people need their egos placating and new matters sometimes have to be discussed by a board. You may have to wait several months to get an answer to your training course requirements – even though it only takes minutes to give someone a direct answer. Unfortunately, businesses procrastinate and drag their feet, particularly larger organisations. This may be because some of those above you in the pecking order are afraid that you may be taking too much initiative, being over-confident or pushy with requests. My advice is to ask nicely and keep on at them. While waiting for an answer, start some other task that needs doing that you can carry out with little or no help.

Larger companies have more departments, so you need to get more involved with them and they need to get more involved with you, especially if you have to ask them to complete new ideas and requests. Be aware, some people do not embrace change readily, even when it is minimal.

When I start systems I go straight to the directors and get their permission to carry out certain acts without delay or extra authorisation. In other words, I build trust with them. That is exactly what you need to do in the first place with your boss; once you do so, the help and resources that you need should follow swiftly.

The other side of the same coin is not to alienate people or ignore them. One day you will need that person's help, advice or information, so stay on good terms with everyone. The last thing you'll need when implementing ISO 9001 is somebody in design being ignored.

If your company carries out design, this is a massive factor in ISO 9001. You will need a lot of time with the design team ensuring that the many sections in design are covered properly. It's all too easy to fall down in this area in ISO 9001, so be careful. Treat everyone well, keep them in the loop and make sure you listen to people of experience. That also goes for any part of the standard and department with which it is applicable.

The last main point I want to make is this: don't introduce paperwork into departments and functions that do not need it. When you are implementing a standard, look at ways in which your company may already comply; in many instances it will do, and this will save you lots of time and effort.

I mentioned exclusions a few paragraphs ago, and I shall cover these in more depth later on. Just to give you an insight, though: you can exclude some parts of ISO 9001 in the standard, but only if you do not carry out what the standard is requesting in section 7. You cannot say you are excluding design because you only design the odd drawing or two a year. More of this in the next section.

To summarise what I have said in this section, you will / may need:

- The best person for the job.

- Good training.

- A good consultant (see section 21).

- An ally and a friend to help you.

If you have all these things in place, you're making very good progress.

7.   Director buy-in, policy and exclusions

I was once on a course at a certification body. We got onto the subject of director involvement and funding in particular. The gentleman sitting next to me was working in the public sector, which as we all know is in the fortunate position of receiving funding from the UK taxpayer.

My acquaintance was completing a project for a local council authority and telling us about his request for a substantial amount of money from his superiors, who were in charge of the finance.

The authority had uncovered the potential for some extra requirements and as it happens, this was to cost in the region of tens of thousands of pounds. After months of protracted debate and deliberation, this council was awarded this substantial sum and the project ran smoothly.

Now imagine you worked in the private sector, went to your directors and said, "Could you fund this ISO project of ours with £XX,000 from your dividends?" "You can just see the director's faces, can't you?

Needless to say, I informed the class that such a request would be utterly ridiculous in the private sector and that the person who made it would be living in "cloud cuckoo land." Only if this was a massive business requirement that was uncovered – only connected to an ISO project by default – would that request gain any credence in the private sector.

The point I'm making is that you should approach a new task or request for cash with caution. Be wary of what you are asking for and try every other route possible before you seek an investment on that scale. Your directors may not always be on board with your ISO wants, but try not to discourage them even further with insane appeals for money. At best, you'll be laughed at and ridiculed if it is over the top. I must add, standards can be implemented with no financial assistance, it just depends on your organisation and people.

The private sector and the public sector are two very different places. Even if you work in the public sector, you won't always be given such sums to play with. Councils are accountable to the taxpayer and money will only be given in exceptional circumstances. (Or so we're told.)

I told this story because it's pertinent to this chapter's subject: director buy-in.

What do we mean by this term? To me, it means that the directors are actively involved with ISO projects and give them their full attention when required. They also provide appropriate resources (within reason).

If you are a director, you probably want to know what you really need to be involved in. Let's break it down.

Firstly, you'll need to oversee a quality policy, section 5.3 of ISO 9001. I'll explain further later on what is involved with this. Secondly, you need to have a management representative to oversee functional responsibility of the project (which could be you or anybody of your choosing; just ensure that the person chosen is the correct choice for your organisation).

Thirdly, you'll need to provide resources for whatever requirements are missing. This could be something such as a training database for your staff or a new computer for the Quality Manager. Resources are covered in more detail below, but briefly: in the eyes of ISO 9001, a resource is something that helps to improve your business and is required by either your business or the quality management standard to ensure that functionality is maintained.

As a director, you should fund (within reason) the attempts to implement a quality management system and the other identified requirements needed to increase your business potential. ISO doesn't tell you exactly what the resources are; that's for you and your business to decide. Just make sure that resources are put in place, within reason and where required or asked for.

As a quick example, if you have no training records and you ignore that fact, on an official external audit you may receive a non conformity for not providing the appropriate resource. I hope that you get the picture: invest in your business and it will pay you back.

It is so important to get directors on board and in line with your thinking. Crucial steps can only be taken with director acceptance and authority. If you are in a large company, say 200 people or more, then a senior manager may be the signatory and act on behalf of a director. However, your requests must be substantially beneficial to the company involved or be quick and easy to implement without a large price tag.

To be honest, a quality management system should not need much financing at all, apart from the certification body or a consultant's costs (if you decide to use one). The best inventions and ideas can usually come from staff resourcefulness producing thought-provoking ideas that can be used within the current business structure.

A database can be written records or completed on a computer software package that the company already has. So try to think what you can use already. Then, as your company and management system progresses, you can perhaps ask for a financial package to help to fund your ISO management. If a system brings value, which this undoubtedly will, then eventually your requests will be met with acceptance rather than derision.

Exclusions from the ISO 9001 standard

If you did not know already, you can exclude your company from certain parts of ISO 9001. If you look in the standard on clause 1.2, it will tell you that this **only** applies to clause 7. Product realization.

It was called product realization because when you are attempting to use a standard in differing languages and cultures, ISO must find a way to use words that are compatible throughout the world. Although product realization may sound confusing to some, it simply means how your product or service is started, processed or carried out, checked and completed. In a nutshell, it is what your company actually *does*. And all companies, irrespective of their sector or country of operation, can apply this standard to their business.

Product realization contains various information and instructions on what you must do to conform to requirements on planning, determining and reviewing requirements, customer communication, design and development, purchasing, control of your service/product, validation of processes (testing or checks to ensure they meet planned requirements), identification and traceability, customer property, preservation of your product and control of monitoring and measuring equipment.

The above information is designed so that if your company does not carry out a particular clause operationally, then it can be excluded from it.

For instance, regarding 7.3 design and development, a company can exclude itself from being audited against clause 7.3 if the company does not design its own products or services. The company then has a genuine reason for not carrying out clause 7.3 in ISO 9001 and it will be excluded from the audit scope.

You cannot absolve yourselves from responsibility, however. If an organisation does carry out design and development, but thinks it's a bit of a 'slack area', then it just cannot drop it from the audit. If your organisation carries out a function, you may have no reasonable grounds for exclusion – because you have a responsibility to your customers. So look at each part of clause 7 and ask yourself if your organisation has grounds for exclusion. The auditor will check exclusions anyway so you will need to discuss it with them.

What does this mean to your certificate? In a word, nothing. Exclusions are not stated on the certificate, so it will make no difference at all. It is an excellent idea to include these exclusions on the part of ISO; if your company has genuine reasons not to do something, they will be accepted and you will not be "punished" by having them written on your certificate.

I shall give you two examples of exclusions that other companies and my own have used. Let me start with my own company bqmc and explain in each case why it is excluded from the clauses.

Example 1: Bqmc

7.5.2 Validation of processes for production and service provision

Bqmc do not validate a system, we audit the systems on behalf of the company as part of our service. It is validated separately by a UKAS / ANAB accredited company for ISO registration.

7.6   Control of Monitoring and Measuring Equipment.

We do not use monitoring and measuring equipment at bqmc.

You can see that our exclusions are simple. Keep it that way in your company, and don't overcomplicate.

Example 2: Atsite.co.uk

7.3   Design and development

Atsite do not carry out design and development of their own products because they purchase all their tools and equipment from other companies. Therefore, they are exempt from that clause.

So using the two examples, you can see where I am trying to lead you. If a company does not carry out a task, it can be excluded.

You will discuss this matter when the external auditors come to visit. Always make them aware of it during the first hour if you haven't already done so.

The auditors will then make their own assumptions, based on your information and their conclusions. If they agree with you, everything will be fine. If s/he thinks that you do not have the grounds for a possible exclusion, then s/he will discuss it with you and make a plan of action. The audit could be ended at this juncture if it is a significant point.

Some of the exclusions are very rare. 7.4 Purchasing is a clause that I have yet to make exclusion for in an organisation. Do you know any companies that don't purchase anything at all? I don't either; and if someone were to ask for exclusion on those grounds, I would end up discussing it at great length with them. The only possible institution that might warrant exclusion for clause 7.4 would be something like a charity, but even they purchase items.

If you only purchase a few items a year, then you would still have to monitor that function. Those two items may be catastrophically important for your company, so it makes sense to include the purchasing function in any quality management system. I recently had someone tell me in all seriousness that they wanted to exclude purchasing. I told them that if you purchase equipment you simply cannot exclude it. The moral is: exclude purchasing from your quality management system at your peril!

One common question I hear is, "Are accounts excluded from audit?" The easy answer is that you do not have to include financial accounts if you do not wish to. ISO 9001 has no interest in your accounting unless you include it as part of your quality system. Not many companies do so. At bqmc, our accounts system is involved in our QMS but only for checks of the system and not for financial scrutiny: I leave that to the taxman and my accountants.

You can include the format of document control of accounts if you so wish, like bqmc does, but that is as far as it should go. Accounts and financial management have been the start of many a dispute. I advise you to not include this area **unless instructed otherwise by the Managing Directors / CEO.**

If you have to, include the financial documents in your register of quality controlled documents for revision and traceability purposes, but that is all.

To summarise, we have covered what the standard lets you exclude and what you yourself should exclude. If there is any doubt, contact a consultant, certification body or a director to assist you. I'm happy to provide free advice by email, so contact me if you have any questions:

contact@bqmc.co.uk

Use of the word "shall" in the ISO 9001 standard

Where you see the word "shall" written in the standard, you **must** comply with what it is saying. If the standard says you *shall* have a documented quality manual, then you will have to have one. If it says you *shall* have a procedure for corrective action, then you must have one of those as well.

There are various places in the standard where the use of "shall" is included. Miss one of these requirements out and you will be heading for a problem on audit. Please read carefully and I will endeavour to point out these pitfalls as we continue.

8.   ISO 9001 implementation and how to approach it

What led me to write this book? Simply that people were coming up to me and saying, "There are no books out there that cut out the jargon and tell you what to do." My aim throughout the writing process has been to provide you, the reader, with a clearer understanding of the ISO 9001 process and how to complete it in your organisation, I hope that you are enjoying it so far.

The worst part about standards is having to translate them into the needs, requirements and the processes of one's business. But often, businesses have a lot of these in place and are surprised at the level of detail they already cover. This book will help you at any stage of implementation – and even beyond that when you have been successfully accredited.

Remember that the standards must be translatable throughout the world; so if you find the terminology confusing, you are probably not alone.

When ISO set out to develop and implement a standard, they have to meet the needs of all countries and overcome language barriers – a truly daunting task. Not surprisingly, some of it may sound a little strange. You need to translate it into your vocabulary and understanding, which is where the skill comes in and this book will help.

That happens to be my speciality. Business people know their own minds but they don't know how to interpret standards. I use their knowledge and encourage openness to find out where their needs lie.

When I implement standards, they are tailored to that organisation. I reject the "one size fits all" approach: in my experience, one size doesn't fit anyone very well!

I help companies by discussing each and every process, and form a proper system of governance that suits them. I do not do shortcuts or introduce a system that isn't incorporated properly. My guess is that you want the same high standards – which is why you're reading this book. In every case, I want to implement a system that adds value to the business and helps with the processes. When I implement management systems, they do all that, encourage proper and effective business building tools and strategies – and come with the invaluable bonus of conforming to international standards.

9.   Your Quality System.

Quality Management System is 4.0 in the standard.

General requirements

General requirements is one of those introductions to the standard which, if you carry out all of the other sections, you don't need to worry about. Having said that, you should be aware of several aspects of this clause.

The information you present should be a part of your quality manual. General requirements is an overview. It will not be a part of a procedure unless you specifically write one for it, put the detail in your manual instead.

If you look at the alphabetical subsections, each one will tell you a different requirement that is necessary to ensure conformity. We'll start with (a). You have to determine the processes in your company that define your quality management system. Start with noting them down. All of your company should be included; if it is not, the scope of your application may be affected. This will need to be discussed with your certificating body.

Now you have written down your processes, you have to determine the interaction and sequence of these processes which is section (b). In this clause it is best to use a diagram, which will help you to fulfil the needs of both (a) and (b) of clause 4.1, and also help you to see how the quality management system should operate in your company. Look at the model of a process-based quality management system in the standard in section 0.2 Process approach, base your system on that and add your company processes in the boxes. If you use Microsoft Visio or a similar package, that will help you to quickly build the process interaction chart for your company. Each of your processes and relevant procedures and what they encompass will fit into the boxes marked "Management responsibility",   "Resource   management",   "Measurement,   analysis   and improvement", "product realization", "Product", "Customers' requirements" and "Customers' satisfaction".

As I mentioned previously, the best place to put all this information is the quality manual. I will explain about the manual in clause 4.2; suffice to say here that your quality manual should describe the overview of the company QMS.

Part (c) of this clause asks you to determine criteria and methods to make sure that the processes and operation of your QMS are effective. As you write your quality manual, use each clause and sub-clause and interpret this information with respect to your company. This should allow you to quickly explain and inform people, staff and to the auditor of how your system works.

With your process interaction chart and further information, you may want to write something like this for section 4.1 in your quality manual:

To achieve our goals, we operate procedures which identify both the processes required and the methods adopted to ensure that the processes are carried out efficiently and effectively.

We operate systems which identify the sequence in which processes are carried out together with consideration of how these processes interact with all other activities.

We have documented systems which identify and ensure that the methods chosen to carry out these processes are effective; and where improvements are made these are documented and again measured for effectiveness by audit and review.

We carry out a regular analysis of the company's resource levels using reviews and audits in order to identify, in a timely manner, where a lack of resource will adversely affect product quality or the level of service that we provide.

We recognise the importance of continual improvement; and all of our procedures have been designed and implemented to ensure that we achieve planned results and maintain an ongoing improvement in all elements of our business.

Because clause 4.1 is very much a "general" overview, try not to worry about it too much. If you have a process interaction chart, describe your company procedures within it and write along the lines I have provided for you. The very fact that you are completing a management system will be enough to cover this clause – if you do what it asks!

In the next part of 4.1, the standard tells you that if you outsource part of your processes that are thought to be of genuine importance to your systems of work, then you must control that outsourcing function. To cut a long story short, you must place quality controls over your suppliers if it is deemed necessary.

If you monitor suppliers, as we will discuss in clause 7.4, you will place them under scrutiny. You cannot absolve any responsibility in quality just because you source a product or service from elsewhere. To control this, you may need to visit them and check that they are operating to your requirements. When I was a quality manager I used to go and visit our suppliers and audit them properly. This ensures that their work met the required standard and that they were following our instructions.

How much you vet them is up to you: but as a general rule, the more complex and important to you their work is, the more involved you want to be. You will have to use your professional judgement based on your company processes.

Documentation requirements

General

When the standard says "general", there is a tendency by people reading it to overlook the requirements.

This clause says that three requirements are needed and it tells you exactly what these are. The beauty of this clause is that it is straight to the point. It informs you (that to pass this standard) you will require a quality policy and company objectives that are encompassed in a documented statement. I shall introduce the requirements of a quality policy and objectives in clause 5.3 in this chapter.

You will also need a documented (hard copy and/or electronic copy) quality manual. The manual is the bread and butter of the quality management system and is the top level document required in your system. The quality manual is one of the most important aspects of the system, alongside your procedures; and is the document that I consider the most important. I shall discuss the quality manual in the next clause, 4.2.2.

This clause also tells you that you will need documented procedures and records. So what are documented procedures and records? For a start you'll need (at the very least) six documented procedures – as well as your quality manual. The procedures are, in no special order: (1) Control of documents (2) Control of records (3) Internal audits (4) Control of non-conforming product (5) Corrective action (6) Preventive action. That might sound an onerous task, but it isn't in practice. The procedures are mandatory in the standard, just as much as the quality manual is, so you cannot excuse yourselves from writing them.

Just for the record, implementing six may get you through the audit; but it is sometimes frowned upon to just do the mandatory minimum number. If your company is relatively complicated, or has lots of departments, you should really write more. The standard asks you to document your main processes, which could involve:

- Human resources and personnel
- Accounts
- IT and information security
- Training and education
- Marketing
- Quotes
- Contract review
- Design and development
- Purchasing
- Goods in/out
- Production
- Sales
- Testing and calibration

Depending upon the complexity of your organisation, you could have more of these. There should be a mix of supporting, realisation (to help to make the product or deliver the service) and organisational procedures.

Procedures can be written with the help of other staff. Get them to help you with their departments, if they know the system better than you do, take advantage of their knowledge; ask them for lots of information to write down. It should not take more than a few hours to write each one. Including the mandatory six procedures, I usually write between 11 and 22 for my clients depending on the size and complexity of their business.

I usually interview people from different departments. I find out what they do; and if necessary, introduce new ideas and methods that will help them to conform to the standard. When you do the same, ensure that you understand the standard as you will be guiding your company. Each part of this book will help you to comply, so try not to worry. Also, when I encounter a clause that requires a mandatory procedure I will say so and inform you of what to write.

Records are what your company uses to gather information. They ensure that your daily operations are recorded with the appropriate information so that evidence is in place for all sorts of uses – including auditing to a standard. The main difference between a record and a document is that the former records information, while the latter holds information that is pre-written or already in place or is ready to accept information - which turns it into a record.

The standard tells you in sub-clause 4.2.1 d) that you will require documents, including records that are needed by your company to ensure that the effective operation and control of your company processes is in order. That basically means everything can come under scrutiny.

Now you have an idea of what's required, let's take a more in-depth look at the quality manual.

Quality manual

Mandatory requirement.

Without doubt, this is one of the most important assets of any quality system. The key to writing this is to read the standard – and be patient. It may take you from one day to several days depending on your experience of writing quality manuals.

You can buy templates of manuals: these can be useful, but you will have to change the template to suit your business. In other words, use it as a basis.

To be compliant, the quality manual must include: the scope of your quality management system (what your business does and where the system applies); what the documented procedures are and where they are applied; and the ways in which the processes interact (in a suitable chart or diagram, as described in Clause 4.1).

In my opinion the quality manual should be about 20-40 pages in depth, depending on the complexity and processes of the business. Not all are, of course; I have audited a quality manual of two pages. Yes, it conformed to the standard, but did I believe the company was serious? No. If the manual presented to me has the required information it will pass the grade; but would you pay a few thousand pounds' consultancy for that and some procedures? It is your choice.

Typically, companies that want the certification done quickly and easily, without fuss or hassle, will take a quick and easy approach. To me, that's a little like passing an exam at school without really understanding the subject. An in-depth approach is about helping the business, about adding value: not just about putting a certificate on the wall. That is why I recommend a detailed and comprehensive manual. My business isn't here to make fast cash, but to offer quality service. If you are serious about your business, I would urge you to invest wisely in your approach, whatever it may involve.

The manual should (in my opinion) tell you what each part of the standard means to your company. Similar to the approach taken in this manual, all you need on each clause and sub-clause of the manual is a few sentences or paragraphs explaining what the standard means to you and your company. What does it involve in your company? This really helps you to focus on the standard and dissect it. The result: you get a far greater understanding of the manual, the processes, and most importantly, the ISO 9001 standard.

As I said, the translation of the language (in the standard) is important. Some of the wording may sound a little strange, because it is written to be understood in over 100 different languages when translated. Don't worry about that: concentrate on getting the text right for your company. A quality manual that is written solely for one company is an incredibly powerful statement on audit. It shows that you care.

Control of documents

This clause requires a mandatory documented procedure and is about how you should control your documentation.

Firstly, it is always a good idea to have a company register of documents. I know that there may be departments or areas in companies where the people have their own methods and formats; but ISO 9001 forces you to standardise these. In an environment where there is quality management, you must all be singing from the same hymn sheet. Make a document register, on Excel or some similar package. Put in the title block (at the top of the page), Document number, name of document, revision (i.e. 1,2,3,4,5 etc) reason for revision (when revised), date of new revision, and the places where this document is used – if your company is large, this will help for traceability purposes when you make a new revision and the documents need changing.

If you don't do this, then your company cannot possibly be one where a quality management system operates effectively. Ideally all documents should come from one controlled source, a person who edits, amends, publishes and controls documents to prevent just anybody in the company changing them to suit themselves. The dangers of that are obvious: people make changes, save them to their desktop and don't tell others what they have done. Then, the auditor finds your documents, realises that there are differing versions and concludes that your documentation process is out of control – which it will be if you allow this to happen.

The natural solution is to control them from source. If different departments have their own, get one of the staff to control that department. You cannot have any form of control if you do not get a grip of your documentation. Some companies look really silly on audit when this happens.

In your procedure, explain how to control and modify all your documentation. The next paragraphs will help you to write it and give you useful insights into what to do.

(A) To approve documents for adequacy you will need to say who does this and what the format is for approval. Are there several people involved in this process, or one? Make sure that you get the responsibilities from others if you need it. Write down how you will approve documents: is it by discussion and immediate publication? Does your MD/CEO need to accept them, does a certain department or person need to have a say? Only you can decide; but my tip is to ask the person who uses that form, and then edit, modify or introduce a document only with their approval.

(B) When you review and update documents, how do you do this? Do you check them regularly, and do you need to? Who does the review involve? These questions are all relevant and will help you to decide your process for review. To make it easy, if you have a document register, you can just scan this and check to see if changes are required and that you are up to date on all of your revisions. If you have a hard copy of each quality document and a register, you can check that all is up to date quickly by just viewing one document at a time at your desk.

(C) When you do make changes and revisions, the best practice is to update your document and the register simultaneously. Always make sure that the revision and date are on the document; these will help with identification. This also ties in with the next point.

(D) All procedures and documents must be available at points of use that are relevant for that department or function. For example, if you have a purchasing procedure, I would expect a purchasing procedure to be present in the purchasing department. If you have a design team, I would expect them to have a design procedure for this function in their office or desk.

Anywhere that has a procedure and documentation to carry out the operational side of the business should have the documents to hand. Leaving work instructions or procedures stuck in a quality management system on a desk or a computer where they are rarely seen is useless.

(E) Your documentation should be readable and authentic. It must be identifiable and if required, recorded in the QMS document register.

(F) Documents of external origin (i.e. your purchased copies of standards, ISO 9001, ISO 14001, etc) should be controlled. The simple practice of including them in your document register, under a separate heading of external documentation, will suffice. This external documentation is applicable to the planning and operation of the quality management system. So you should record your copy of ISO 9001 on your register. If you have more than one copy, please explain and include where it has been distributed to.

(G) It can be difficult to prevent the unintended use of documents if you do not operate this controlling point properly. If you have a register and the hard copies, you will find your control is easier. If you distribute electronically you can easily update a revision. Take the old revision, "save as" an archived document after its electronic title and make a new folder on your server/pc called "Quality documents archive." This will enable you to put your old revisions in the archive and keep your new revision where it should be – and also eliminates problems arising from people using older documents.

When you make a revision, please ensure that the department is updated. Remove old copies and replace them with new revisions. If you do this it keeps everybody in the loop and happy.

To save space, recycle the old paper revisions or shred them depending on their security status. Just keep the old electronic copy in the archive for information and if asked by an auditor. One day someone will ask, so keep your archive up to date.

My last tip is, when you make a revision, complete the whole revision process there and then for that one document. Because if you do not, the chances are that you will forget. If you have 100 documents and you needed to amend one throughout the year and fail to do it properly, you can bet that the auditor will find it!

Control of records

This clause requires a mandatory documented procedure.

If you remember the distinction I made between documents and records, you'll see that this is a different subject to the previous clause. Your records are the operational data you input into your documents. The two work together, so keep records – and ensure they are retrievable.

Records *are* your company, they make your business tick, they are there to prove your worth and your product. Without them, what is there to audit? How can you control your data?

You need to take the following into account when writing your procedure and deciding what controls you need for your records.

How does your company identify records? This is much the same as for documents. The record is written on the document, so if the document is controlled then it is identifiable.

Storage: where do you store these records and documents? Is it on a pc, in a file, where are they likely to be found? You do not have to go into specifics but a company overview will be necessary.

Protection: how do you intend to protect your records? Is there password control? Are people keeping records under lock and key or in certain places? All this needs to be described.

Retrievable: how are records retrieved in your company? Where are they? Are there any controls for retrieval?

Retention: make sure that you put down what your retention format is, document how many months/years you intend to keep your quality and other records for. You may want to include accounts records, health and safety records, and environmental records. Whatever you do, make sure quality and health and safety records are top of the list and you specify how long you are retaining them.

Another important aspect is how you back up your records. Most companies now use a personal computer, laptop etc. A lot of companies fail to back up their systems – which is a catastrophe waiting to happen. You should ensure that all your company records are backed up on a separate storage device or two. This is as true for one-man bands as it is for huge conglomerates.

I have seen grown men cry because of lost electronic data. I have also known yearly accounts be lost because of a back-up failure. Not surprisingly, the company or person affected never does it again, and back-ups are always in good order from then on. But doesn't it make sense to do it now, before a crisis forces you to change your ways?

I once came across a company that carried out back-ups and thought they were working perfectly – until I asked to see the evidence. It turned out that the device had become faulty and their records hadn't been backed up for over a year. Make sure you check the hard evidence, go into a file or two and retrieve the data to see if it actually works correctly. If it doesn't, get it repaired without delay.

The auditor should ask if you make back-ups and may ask to see evidence. Your back-ups could be on an internal server, external server, cloud computing, extra hard disks, other media such as tapes, CDs, memory sticks, etc. This is such an important area of business and in this procedure you should explain how your company makes back-ups of its data and records.

What constitutes a quality record?

Quality plans, management review minutes, internal audits, corrective action plans, training and personnel files, measurement notes, receipts, invoices, purchase orders, despatch notes or collection notes, calibration notes, risk assessments, method statements: any company-controlled document that may have data written onto it for any business purpose. This is an example list, you may have more or less than this.

What you cannot do is say that your risk assessments are not included, or your purchase logs. You can't exclude documents in your organisation; if you are implementing a quality management system, your company records are everything. You may be able to exclude parts of clause 7 but you are not allowed to pick and choose what paperwork the auditor wants to check.

I deem a record as any company document that holds information of any kind, whether it has one line of information or over a hundred lines. Records are there to prove to the auditors that you have matters under control.

Now we have covered section 4, it is now time to move onto section 5. Management responsibility is a subject that some companies overlook, make sure that you get management involved and don't do all of the hard work yourself.

10. Managing effectively and responsibly

Management Responsibility is 5.0 in the standard

Senior management must ensure that they provide evidence of their commitment to the implementation, management and development of a quality management system by communicating requirements and the importance of meeting all regulations, both customer, statutory and other. They must ensure that a quality policy is established, ensure that quality objectives are calculated and promoted, conduct management reviews and make the necessary resources available. These are necessary to complete the QMS in their companies and to ensure that resource levels are maintained for any future requirement.

I will concentrate on quality policy in 5.3; but for now, just be aware that you will need one. Quality objectives are also discussed in 5.4.1, Quality objectives are company objectives or key performance indicators that enable the measurement of something important. This is another area that I feel is lacking in a lot of companies when I audit them.

Management reviews are required (discussed in 5.6) as are availability of resources, (in 6.2).

5.1 is a general overview, where, if you implement every clause and sub-clause in clause 5, it will be totally taken care of.

Management responsibility and commitment is a clause that always makes me smile. Why? Because commitment is not defined by depth in the standard, it is defined by allocating responsibility and resource. I believe that this part of the standard should go further and introduce mandatory controls that would force directors to be more meaningfully involved and responsible to the system.

During my audits and consultancy, I notice that lots of directors palm off their responsibility, especially in management reviews and matters concerning the system.

69

When I wrote a quality management system for a company, I scheduled the management review three times – and each time it was cancelled because we couldn't get the directors to commit to the meeting. Obviously, it wasn't important to them. I had to write the review as though we had had a meeting, print it off and hand it to them instead. So if you're a director, please give this area the time and the commitment it calls for. It only takes an hour a year.

The management section is vital because it is the senior management who fund the system. Maybe because of this, directors think that they do not require any further commitment or are "too busy and important" to have any thorough involvement. Well, they are wrong.

If you have directors that "just want the system in place", tell them that you are trying to add value to the business and it is important that they attend to their responsibilities. If they cannot make a meeting, postpone it until they can attend, or, when they have cancelled for the third time, do it all yourself and look for a better job elsewhere.

The reason ISO dedicated a whole section to management responsibility is to try and force the senior managers to take a hands-on approach, but as I said, this doesn't go far enough. Management commitment should have a clause in it called "active participation of directors" and a way forward should be forged in the next edition of ISO 9001 to force more meaningful involvement from the top.

The other side of the coin to this argument is that if something does go wrong, people and managers are quick to blame the QMS Representative. Blame in companies is usually shared. I have known quality managers to be scared stiff of major (critical) nonconformities; but it should not be like that. The quality management system is everyone's responsibility, not just one person. Having said that, the quality representative of a company needs to ensure that they are doing their job correctly if they are to raise points of order or argue their cause on an issue of irresponsibility.

In the standard it mentions top (senior) management. That means directors and those managers involved in high-level decision making. Make your managers aware of clause 5 and inform them of their responsibilities, even if it is by email or printed memorandum!

I cannot stress enough how much it helps to have director and senior management involvement. As I mentioned previously, if you have the backing and commitment of at least one director, your job becomes easier. Not only is it a great way of building trust and comradeship, it is important to have someone as "a go-to" in times of stress and need. If you need something, they can help, if you are having trouble with a quarrelsome member of the team who does not like change very much, they can help. If you need another director's input and involvement, they can help.

If you're a director who is inclined to take a back seat whilst it is incorporated, remember that your "responsible person" will bring your company value, recognition and set you on a course for excellence that will be recognised worldwide. What better way of improving your profits, reputation and standing than by having an internationally recognised business system in place! So get off the fence – and get involved.

Customer focus

Customer focus is tied with 7.2.1 and 8.2.1, which will be discussed later.

What is customer focus in our eyes? It is ensuring that your customers are kept in the loop, satisfied and well served. Without customers, there is no business.

The ISO wants businesses to focus on customer needs; it recognises that where customers are cared for and their needs concentrated on, businesses are far more likely to develop well and ensure that quality controls are put into place. If a business was insular and looked after only its own needs, then a customer may not get proper service. Hence this part of the standard.

So what should your company be doing to ensure that your customers are happy? To begin, a company must have dialogue with its customers. This can be interpreted differently for each company. For example, let's consider a pharmaceutical company developing drugs for patient use. In this case, hospital trusts, doctors and consultants would want to be kept in the loop regarding products that may be given to their patients. They could do this by test analysis, asking about side effects and monitoring symptoms and causes. Records would indicate issues or any problems or side effects in different people.

What about a retail company? They should be asking customers how their products perform. They could send out a questionnaire, either written or online. They could ask people when they came into their shops. How do you get people to fill these valuable bits of information in? Give them a prize, of course. Such feedback helps companies to improve their operations and become more profitable.

Let's look at an engineering firm. The managers here need to talk to their customers to see how their products or services are performing. Is technical data available? Is there detailed analysis of mechanical calculations, do the beam calculations require slight changes, is the pressure vessel strong enough?

Lastly, what about a college? They should be asking students on courses and content. What would help students study more effectively?

A company that engages with customers is forward thinking. It welcomes positive and negative feedback to help it to improve: and the more constructive it is, the better.

Companies that don't welcome feedback are, in my opinion, arrogant if they don't have good reason for engaging with their customers. I ask my clients every consultancy day if they are happy. Good feedback helps me to improve my service; it also adds extra value to my clients and keeps them in the process.

Always be aware that a customer needs to be valued, I value what people think of this book, again with the proviso that it's constructive. I'm interested in thoughts for the future and welcome new ideas.

The ISO put this into the standard because they know that it is a massively important step to gain feedback from customers. This is another area which I feel could be improved at companies.

The ideas for your businesses are: online questionnaires, feedback forms, telephone interviews and direct questions when you are with them. Use these to gain feedback: your customers will feel valued and will welcome your approach.

Quality Policy

The quality policy (mandatory requirement) is one of the fundamental aspects of ISO 9001 and a quality management system. Some overlook its importance but I for one see it as the top-level document alongside the quality manual.

Your quality policy should be tailored to your company and explain what your business is involved in. At the start, your policy should say what you do and explain your desire for improvement through a quality management system.

As the standard says, it should be appropriate to your organisation. In other words it is not a template, it hasn't come from somewhere else; it is yours and it has a good company feel to it.

Secondly it should have an organisational commitment to continual improvement, the proof of which, shall be in your management system in the form if taking action and records of this.

Thirdly, it should mention legal and contractual responsibilities and that you are abiding by them.

The policy should provide a framework for establishing and reviewing quality objectives. This means that you discuss company objectives with senior management (directors) and document them in the policy. I expect to see some quality goals on a policy to make it authentic, and it needs to be assessed yearly to maintain credibility. Discuss goals at management review, write a new policy and include them: there is your framework. You can also audit it to see how far your previous goals have progressed.

It does not necessarily matter if your goals were not reached, as long as you know the reason. Just try to improve your business further by using sensible goals for you and your employees to focus on.

The policy should be communicated and understood throughout your company. In other words it should read well in your chosen language, be clear, not contain too much jargon and involve the entire organisation.

If the policy is bespoke, has two, three or four (or more if you wish) well defined goals, you have identified that you will abide by legal and other, plus contractual requirements, has the expected statements of commitment to continual improvement and to continually improve the system, has a framework for review and is available upon request to your customers and clients etc, then you are on the right track.

Quality objectives

Quality objectives are simply goals. What do you wish for in a quality management system? Is it business progress, better management, documented processes and visibility? Do you want to achieve professional recognition, or win more business from existing and potential clients? Perhaps a local authority has asked you to consider ISO 9001 as part of a tendering process? Is it to achieve more money? Higher profits? The list is endless.

What you and your company have to decide is exactly what are you trying to achieve. What is ISO 9001 going to help you to do? Where is it pushing you? Do you welcome ISO 9001 in your business and if so, what will it do for you?

These are all simple questions for you to ask yourself what you want out of this system. If you are implementing a quality management system on behalf of a company, have you asked the directors what they want out of it?

If your directors only want this as a prerequisite to some further business and are not excited about implementing this standard, you may have trouble getting decent information out of them. That's because if ISO implementation is seen as a necessity rather than an opportunity, people are often reluctant to enter into the spirit of the system in general.

If this is the case and your senior managers are only interested in you completing this without the hassle, this is what you should do. First, use your imagination and don't set your sights too high. If you are subordinate to somebody, they may think that you are getting ahead of yourself, so tread with care.

What can you help the business to achieve? Your processes may require mapping and to give your company greater understanding of its workings, in this case a quality goal (objective) would be:

(1) To assist in the mapping of our company processes to improve efficiency.

Another objective could be to gain a local authority or council contract. The objective would look like this:

(2) To assist the company to achieve two contracts with the local authority.

Finally you could choose something to do with customers. This could be improving your dialogue and feedback from your customer base. You must decide who you are going to contact and how may surveys you are going to send. A goal could then be set as:

(3) Send one in 10 customers a satisfaction survey and achieve an average score of 20 / 25 on five items (that you wish to improve), scored from 1 to 5 for each item.

Hopefully you can see what I'm getting at. It doesn't have to be complicated; you can discreetly carry out what you need to do without annoying people. And if you help the company to improve, you may get a raise!

If you are in a company where the senior management are involved and happy that the system is being put in, ask them their goals and aspirations for the company. It can get quite exciting seeing a company get closer to its goals.

Before we move on, let me just say that anyone who thinks that goals are unimportant is mistaken. Goals are a rudder to your aspirations, in business and in personal life. If you have no goals, what is the point in anything? Where does the direction come from? For instance, consider the difference between "I'd like to write a novel one day" and "I will write one chapter of a novel each week for the next six months." Don't plod away, set worthwhile goals – and it's amazing what can be achieved.

The standard says that the quality objectives should be consistent with the quality policy. The easiest and best thing to do is to include them in your policy, audit them and discuss them at management review meetings.

Objectives (goals) in a policy make it look authentic, give the policy credence and help it to be taken seriously when scrutinised by an external auditor. If your objectives are commensurate with your policy and your quality system, you will be fine, try to keep them up to date at least yearly. There is nothing worse on audit having goals on a policy that are 2 or 3 years old.

The next step is to make sure that you are monitoring your objectives. You can do this by graphs (on Microsoft Excel or word), you can complete graphical data on a spreadsheet or a word package, or use one of the many other ways to do this.

If you are completing customer surveys, you may want to write the returned results down in a table. This will prove that the objectives are being taken seriously, since an objective is of no use if you are not measuring it. It will also tell you how far you are from reaching your targets.

Quality management system planning

This part of the standard is one of those that will take care of itself on thorough implementation.

In my opinion, it is something of a misnomer. If you are carrying out an implementation task, you will surely plan it first. Planning a management system should be relatively straightforward. How should you start?

First, write down the major areas of the business. These could be purchasing, goods inward/outward (despatch), maintenance, manufacture (of whatever it is you are selling), calibration, security of systems, testing, reviewing, customer service, and so on.

You can of course do it by process. If so, try to document the main areas of the company. This helps you focus on those processes that are the most important for your business. Also, the standard does not ask you to map all of them. The mandatory procedures are six in total.

Next, plan the quality policy as previously discussed and look to add extra control where it may be needed. Beware though, as I said previously, tread carefully and ask nicely, do not make demands, or use the standard as an excuse to get your way. Treat people in other departments with respect and ask them in a professional manner: this will involve meetings, constructive dialogue and above all, a progressive attitude. Remember that people are resistant to change so if you are introducing new planning methods and structures, don't be surprised if people do not want to alter their systems of work. Nevertheless, the integrity of the system must not be compromised just because someone doesn't want change. Whatever barriers you face, overcome them with friendliness (and perhaps a little guile).

Always keep in the back of your mind when introducing systems and planning, that ISO or British Standard implementation is about "fitting the standard to the business" – not the other way round. There is a world of difference. If you have a business method that works, you are in control of it, maybe you just need to apply a few finishing touches? Most companies that I come across need the following as an example: a quality manual and procedures, a brush up on customer service, customer records need tighter security, tools need calibrating and controlling, the personnel training records need updating, they need their audits and an audit schedule completing and their management review. Some obviously need a lot more; and a few need less than that and are in near complete control.

Control of your business is good. Control is vital for success; many companies do not plan or control, which is planning to fail. Where there is no control, expenditure goes up, confidence goes down and spirals of complacency can occur.

Controlling a system and planning are key areas of business. Why do some companies not do this? Perhaps because they either think they are above a standard and planning and just go by their intuition; maybe they are unaware of the support and help out there; or perhaps they think that it is too expensive. This system of work brings out-and-out value when done correctly and it need not always involve extra expense, maybe just the expertise from your staff and a little efficiency.

However, do not tinker with what works by trying to introduce new methods unnecessarily. That is "fitting the business to the standard". The key to implementation is finding out where the standard already fits, not by working out what new methods you can bring just for the sake of it, which will just annoy people.

There are complete systems out there that you can purchase. These can be of value — if you are lacking in complete structure for your business. For some, these are crucial pieces of work, but if that system is on a sole computer and that system is removed or stolen, what ISO 9001 system do you have in your company? Correct, none. Make sure you have back ups.

Full ISO or British Standard implementation is about the business, not a system that just hides away in some discreet file or folder, just to get a certificate.

This system is about the whole organisation and the whole organisation is about your business. Never forget that. That is why you fit the standard to the business, because the business comes first. If you fit the business to the standard then you may change your systems for the worse or add items that are not needed — something which doesn't tend to impress directors.

The main aspect of all this is, read the standard and try to interpret it for your business so that you do not go over the top with your implementation.

To get the planning correct, you must aim to get everybody on board. Depending on the size of your company you can have meetings and get people around the table and map this out.

I feel that a great deal of dialogue is missed out with these systems, and that is a problem. To get around this, speak to people and get everyone involved. This will make them far more inclined to help you, and your task of planning the implementation will be much easier.

Responsibility and communication

Responsibility and authority

To start with, responsibility is vested in the person(s) that are carrying out the task of ISO 9001 implementation and/or quality control.

Top management must ensure that whoever is carrying out the task is doing a good job of it and completing it correctly. This area of the standard is one that I feel needs bringing out a bit more to assist the implementer who is not necessarily a senior manager.

Some organisations are not really involved. They want the outcome – the tick in the box, the UKAS, IAF or ANAB certificate – without the effort. Responsibility and authority are about leading by example, so if you are a director, ensure that you do so. If you are passing that responsibility to a colleague, give them the necessary support.

On internal audits I could have given many an organisation a non-conformance on this area. I went to one company for an audit and it took them a full hour to find the quality manual. Shocking. I asked the Managing Director why this was the case, he said that he only wanted the tick in the box because a customer demanded it of his company.

These companies do not realise that the systems are not just there for the "tick in the box", they bring value and control. Even though some of these companies want them just for the above, they don't realise that they add value without them noticing. They keep them in check.

Responsibility needs to be communicated and defined, as requested in the standard. It is sensible mentioning in your quality policy how you are going to communicate the quality system.

Management representative (MR)

The management representative should be named in the quality manual as the person who has complete responsibility for the system and they should be named (with title) on the company organisation chart. If you don't have one then you can easily do this on Microsoft Visio or Word.

The MR, as I shall call him or her, has a great responsibility to the company. They must ensure that all of the processes are mapped correctly and that the full task of the implementation as required by the standard is in place in the business or is about to be fitted to it if something is missing.

The MR needs to report to and liaise with the senior management to keep them in the loop. Ensure you ingratiate your ideas with your peers and bosses because you will need their support at certain times.

ISO implementation can cause conflicts. The best advice that I can pass to the MRs is to be diplomatic, honest, and have integrity. Ensure that what you're asking for needs to be done, not because you want to change some part of the business for personal reasons.

I go into lots of companies and it can get quite uncomfortable, especially those with little cliques and groups of friends. There are always egos to placate and people to assuage. I met one company that never spoke to its customers, so I introduced a new method for them. "We're not doing that, it doesn't suit our business," they said. I said, "That's fine; please do something else then. But one thing is for sure: if you don't speak to your customers, you will not be getting a certificate!"

As an MR, you have to be strong and firm with your requests – as long as they are backed up with a credible reason and you are not asking for the directors to pay the earth to make changes.

As the MR, you must liaise with other companies' quality representatives, especially if you are in manufacturing or pharmaceutical or something that involves great customer dialogue. Be prepared for company trips out.

You must liaise effectively with other companies because their quality as a supplier will affect your quality: and if non-conformances are delivered to your company, then it is your responsibility to deal with them and ensure that a swift and appropriate response is generated.

The other part of your responsibilities is to ensure that every person in your company is aware of what is going on with your quality management system. This leads us nicely to the next part of the standard.

Internal communication

This is an easy one – or it should be! The first thing you should think about is that although you may like to keep your quality management system to yourself, "knowledge is power and all that", this will only work if you are the only person in your business!

Internal communication is about letting everyone know about your QMS. Where will that start? First, I'd suggest that you get your quality policy on the walls and around everyone's workplace. You do not have to do this, but how else are you going to communicate your system and goals if you just keep them in your quality manual and only the directors and MR's get to see them?

At the very least, I would have a quality policy in each place of work in your business. Although many people will ignore it, many will not and will pay great interest to it. They may want to help you and will want to ensure that the company meets its goals.

Communication can of course be carried in various ways: orally, memos, notice boards, email, SMS, Twitter, Facebook, etc. This is the modern age, the technological age, and some people may choose these methods. I welcome any way of improvement and communication. Communication is a powerful tool, and it should be maximised.

One important issue you should communicate is procedures. If you have a procedure that belongs in Purchasing and is only in your Quality Management System file, then they need one in purchasing. Similarly with despatch, sales, etc. If you have a procedure for different departments, make sure that they can access them either electronically or they have an up-to-date hard copy for reference.

Internal communication is important. You need to tell people about updates, news of internal and external certificating audits, management reviews, corrective actions, proposals, preventive actions, problems with suppliers or products, problems internally and products to look out for and check. The list is endless.

Just make sure that you communicate well and your job and task will get easier. The more you keep to yourself, the less successful you will be. The reason's not hard to find; people love to be kept in the loop, even if they are not really interested. If you keep them updated, when you ask for their help they are more inclined to give you some assistance.

When I come in as an auditor I always ask people where the quality policy is. If three or more people haven't a clue, I may enquire as to why and may raise a non-conformance on this part of the standard. Too many companies fail at not getting across the policy properly and it is just stuck in some file somewhere – where it might as well not exist.

The standard refers to communication of the effectiveness of the quality management system. If you write an email or memo to everyone or write a notice and put it in a prominent position in the organisation, that is good practice.

Effectiveness is measured in a variety of ways. Is your system effective? Does it need improvements? Is everything well at present? How did the audits go? These are many points that you can mention.

Management review, review input and review output

First things first: management reviews are carried out when *you* specify. Most organisations put this into their system. I believe that one review a year is sometimes not enough but is about the average. But some organisations I go to don't even carry it out that frequently – and end up with a non-conformance because their procedure says that they do complete one every year! Management review is absolutely necessary.

You need to do the review at planned intervals, and write what the interval is in your quality manual. Planned intervals are how you interpret the importance of the quality management system in your business and how involved and effective it is for you. This will be reflected by the frequency of your review: if you think that the system is very important you may do one every three or six months, if you are less involved it will be twelve months (and if you couldn't care less, it will be once every eighteen months or even less frequently).

If you go for longer than twelve months, beware: auditors may probe the depths of your organisation and may possibly look for an issue or two to raise against you. Not because they can but because a review at least annually is a sort of unwritten rule; and if you go over that then you may be taken with less seriousness? Let's be honest, completing something which takes maybe a couple of hours once a year is not difficult.

Records from the review must be kept. One page of scribble is not good enough for the review. This is about business progression and the review concentrates on areas that are important. If you feel that the review is unnecessary then you must change your tack.

Reviews are the basis of improvement, a measuring stick to gauge yourselves against. They highlight problems to be resolved – and more importantly give other people the responsibility for action instead of putting it all on the management representative.

The management review is the chance for you as MR to prioritise actions, to get a varied mixture of company involvement, gain acceptance for planning and new resources, get extra support and get other people to carry out tasks instead of doing it all yourself.

This review is crucial for the MR. Quite simply because it is here that you can get your wishes, resources, financial support and the ear of the directors. This is your chance to speak, so plan effectively and make your mark count.

If you get acceptance and authority to progress on some matters, that can be very exciting and also the review can get someone to carry out something on your behalf. Remember that this is a joint effort; you are the facilitator, not the only one with responsibility.

When you plan the review, look at the standard and check what is required in 5.6. It tells you what is expected. So it makes sense to use the points in 5.6.2 and 5.6.3 as the agenda. Many companies add to these; but you must cover the elements required and using the points is an excellent way of doing so.

You can change the headings slightly to suit your company. If you do so, why not place the item on the standard in brackets next to it? This way the auditor will know exactly what you are covering.

Follow-up actions from previous reviews are only necessary if you have carried out a previous review. If this is your first, just mention in the minutes that this is your first review and you will be using the recorded minutes as a basis for follow-up at the next management review.

When you are planning the review, you must get results to discuss, you must have detail.

Let's take customer feedback for instance. If you have no records, what are you going to say? What are you going to improve? Remember, the idea of a QMS is to make continuous improvements.

If you have measured your feedback at 55 per cent, how are you going to improve it, by what method? Who is in charge of customer service? What have they to say about it? What is the next improvement step and what is the timeframe? What is your next goal? 60 per cent, 70 per cent? It's up to you: but you need to decide how you are going to reach that goal, who is responsible for each task, and so on. There is so much value to add to your review and so much to discuss.

This part of the standard is self-explanatory and is easy to follow. The guideline that I have previously given to you on customer feedback is a great example to follow and will give you food for thought on each subsection.

Sub section (d) is about corrective and preventive actions; this part can be amalgamated into all the other sub-sections. Each sub-section will require actions to carry out, so under each one, have a space for actions and another for the timeframe and responsibility for the required action that you have all agreed upon.

If you have the unenviable task of doing the review by yourself because you are in a one or two-person business, do the review once a year and complete as much of it as you can. Write the sub-sections and try to stay focused: this system will be well worth it when you grow and you have all of your processes mapped out.

When I completed my company's system I had been trading for eight months and it was just me. Later on, other people joined the company and knew exactly what was needed and how things stood. Thanks to my work, the processes were visible, the procedures were in place.

If you are doing it by yourself in a company of many people and many directors (many means more than five people and one director or more) and people are not interested, stick up for yourself if people will not attend. It is your responsibility to carry out the review when everyone is available though. So don't organise it when you know that some people are away. Get everyone together and if someone excuses themselves at the last minute, progress with the meeting anyway. Show them that you are busy and that this work is just as important as they are.

Now you have your documentation completed and the management part of it is coming to fruition, lets get cracking with the resources part of the standard

11. Managing resources effectively

Resource management is 6.0 in the standard.

Provision of resources

This part of the standard highlights resources. What are resources? The answer is anything that is helping a business to build itself.

Resources are people, training programmes and education, devices, equipment, tools, electrical programmes, printers, telephones and software etc... pretty much anything that the business needs to make itself tick over. For this standard, make sure that you have the tools for effective quality management system implementation. It's down to the company to plan and make provision for effective resources, maybe you'd like to send someone on an auditors course to help your company too?

The company has to enhance customer satisfaction by meeting customer requirements. In other words the company must ensure that it has "the tools to do the job" to keep your customers pleased and happy that your products and services are up to scratch.

The company also has to ensure that its quality management system is effective that it is and continually trying to improve it. The worst thing a company can do is rest on its laurels about its quality system. It has to prove that in years to come, it isn't just regurgitating audits and management reviews gone by, by just using the same procedures and information that it has used previously. The company has to prove its worth by adding value and continually keeping it on the road of improvement – and that means extra resources where appropriate.

Human resources

General

When your personnel are carrying out tasks on behalf of the company, would you educate them appropriately or just not bother and let them learn "on the job"?

It all depends on what they are doing. Anyone should be able to sweep up or clean, but can they manufacture a part correctly? Can they supervise their own work? Are they qualified in a certain sector such as welding? These are all concerns that are raised during the auditing of a quality management system.

Your company must ensure that all personnel are either educated/trained correctly. Do they have the correct experience? Are they fit for the task and able to carry out your demands at certain times or for hours in the day? Are they correctly educated in their specific fields and do they require monitoring or supervising?

There are all sorts of things to consider. Of course, recruitment is highly important when hiring the people to carry out your tasks. Personnel have to be competent, and that competency is up to you. How do you measure your competency? Is it against a job description or company requirement? Is it recorded? Does the person know what skills are required? Do you let them loose on your products before you have trained them? Whatever it is, you must ensure that they are able to do the job.

If personnel cannot do the job or are not educated correctly, your customers' quality will suffer. You should have a job description or a written piece of documentation explaining what is required of your recruits. If you do not tell people what their job characteristics are, how are they supposed to do the job correctly?

You really need only a sheet of A4 paper and someone with the competence to work it out. Job descriptions are not mandatory for the standard but they certainly help! Give your personnel written processes too. If professional qualifications are involved, then they will be expected to be seen on audit.

I come across many companies that do not have job descriptions at all. I asked one MD what a certain person who worked for him actually did. He said that he didn't really know. I said that I would ask her. When she came in, I said "Can I ask you a few questions as I am trying to map the process of your business please?'" She agreed, and I asked her what she did at the company. She laughed nervously, then told me that she just did 'this and that' with clients' contracts and called them up when they owed money. You could not make it up.

What are you paying people for? Not to sit around and have a laugh, surely? But this person had no job description, no guidance and no common sense either. Unfortunately, directors sometimes cannot see what is happening.

In some companies, staff are on Facebook, on Twitter, sending emails to friends, checking out or buying things online, and gossiping. Is this how your businesses are run? Do you know what your staff are doing? Do they know what you want them to do? Job descriptions, training where necessary, involvement, discipline and procedures will help you. For example, it's reasonable that staff should send emails, but not post on or read Facebook in the office if its personal stuff, unless you are not that bothered? If that's your policy, tell them so.

Competence, training and awareness

How competent should your staff be? The very first question you must address is, how do your staff affect product quality in the workings? Or in other words, what do they do in your process? Are they engineers? Are they machine operatives? Are they support staff / administration? Are they in the stores? Are they directors? Are they managers? Do they have contact with the product?

You have to place an importance against the level of input that the person has into your product. The more input they have, the more training and experience they should have and receive.

If an operative is in quality control, do you think that they should have 30 minutes training? No, I don't think so. They should receive much more. You just have to decide how much more.

To help you to decide, have a scale of 1 - 5, 1 meaning no input to product quality or the process at all, to 5 being extremely important to the process / product quality. If you assign a number to each job in conjunction with other staff and managers, you can decide what level of training they should have. You can look at the level of training related to the post and decide on extra training depending on the person and their current and previous experience.

Of course, you shouldn't run to the bosses demanding extra training for all, but you should highlight areas of weakness and possible areas of improvement. As an example, if you have a quality manager with no qualifications in auditing or the standard that you are implementing, it would be a good idea to get some training organised for him. His work directly affects quality because he oversees the company quality system and also because he will be in charge of inspection, etc.

What you shouldn't do is ask for extra training where it is not necessary. Please do not use ISO standards as an excuse to further your training requirements. They should be in place anyway. However if you do need some extra training, this can be an excellent way of getting some leverage with the bosses.

Training should be carried out that is commensurate with the level of involvement that your staff have with the product that you are selling. The more involved then the greater their training or experience may need to be? Staff should also be aware of the effect of their post and the relevance and contribution to quality and product activities with respect to the organisation.

If we take an example, if you want a quantity surveyor for your business, he or she must already be trained, or undergoing on-the-job and part-time college training subject to in-house guidance too.

If staff do not have the required skill level, then on audit that will be scrutinised and this could lead your company open to potential non-conformities.

If you are implementing the system you really should have at least a few day's training, I will cover training providers later on; but for now, a two-day course in internal auditing or awareness of a standard will certainly help you. If you are carrying out your own internal audits then you will definitely need some training. You could use someone else in the company to do this for you if they have been trained already.

Databases or record keeping is so important in this area. It is vitally important that you keep the appropriate records of training and competency of your personnel.

You will always have to demonstrate competency in a variety of areas in your company. One of the most fundamental and most critical areas are with your staff. They have to be competent and you will have to prove it.

What should you do? For a start, you must have the evidence that your staff are adequately and appropriately educated and trained in their respective positions. The database and/or records need to provide objective evidence that your personnel are up to the task. Of course, training may not always be the most important aspect. This is where experience is the key. Training that has been completed over a number of years may count towards proving effective competency. A database is not mandatory in the standard but it will certainly help you to locate records quickly and easily.

If you have staff with a high degree of experience in their positions, you need to have this detail available as well if their education is lacking. I come across this all the time: people are well trained but have no formal qualification. This is not a problem but you will still have to provide evidence of experience. Some of the best workers I have ever come across hold no formal qualification, so it is a great idea to note experience too. Maybe hold CV's from your staff to assist you with this.

Experience can of course be proven by records, interviews, application forms, CV's etc and is an area that must not be overlooked. If I was auditing a company and they could not provide me with the appropriate training records (and certificates), then I would look to the expertise of that person and their experience before calling judgement against the auditing standard.

Databases are used very regularly, but records are also important in proving your staff's competency. Databases are an easy way of recording information that should be quick to retrieve. If the company is large and personnel are spread about many departments and sites, then you'll need the help from others.

Other people and staff can help you to attain information that you may not be able to retrieve yourself. As I have said previously, make sure that you get other people onside: it is vital in this standard. If you need to bring a company with many departments together, get representatives to note other department's training requirements and records.

Personnel areas are usually audited at or near to the end of the day on the audit. The reason for this is because your personnel will be spoken to throughout the audit, their names and their jobs will be noted. Near to the end of the audit, the auditor will go to the personnel department and ask to see the records of the individuals that they have interviewed and spoken to.

If I am auditing and have twenty names at the end of the audit, then I may sample fifteen of those and check to see that records are intact, training requirements are being noted and adhered to and that experience is fitting where the training was lacking. If I saw that the records are in place and I was given confidence that the staff were trained, educated and performing as required, then the sample audit would be a success in this area at that time. I'll be sure to check again when I visit next year or in six months, whatever your surveillance audit timeframe is? A surveillance visit is when your progress is checked upon by the certificating body.

Infrastructure

The organisation's infrastructure is a very important part in ISO 9001. What is the infrastructure of your company and what does it involve? This is an open question and alters from business to business. You have to ensure that the assets that you use to make your product or service run correctly are themselves up to date and fully functioning.

Infrastructure can apply to a building, room, piece of equipment e.g. computers, software, hardware, lathe, miller, welding machine, laser printer, software, tools for the task, your workspace, utilities, transport and company vehicles, communication devices, laptops, mobile telephones or information systems, air conditioning and temperature control (if required)...the list is huge.

All of the above can apply to many organisations. Obviously all that I have listed may not be relevant to yours, but some of it may. There also may be many pieces of equipment that I have not included that you may have that need to be included. An asset list or register can help you to organise where everything is and control it too. Although not used in the ISO 9001 standard, it *is* used in the ISO 27001 standard, it really can help you to control your assets well and identify with who looks after them or who is responsible.

The pieces of equipment and buildings that you identify are your infrastructure as well. This needs to be considered when applying a management standard.

What do you need to do about it? Firstly you must assess what pieces of equipment require testing and regular maintenance to keep your operation running smoothly. If you are in engineering this may be welding equipment or grinding machinery. It could be process plant or an accurate jig that work needs to fit to. Anything can be included if it is important to the quality of your processes that does not come under the similar clause of monitoring and measuring equipment in clause 7.6. There is a fine line between some equipment mentioned in 7.6 and the assets mentioned in 6.3.

95

To divide them, if it monitors or measures then it comes under clause 7.6. If it is something else, like a welder or a lathe, portable electrical items, or a milling machine or perhaps a computer, then it comes under 6.3. If it monitors as well (i.e. a computer), just make sure that the equipment is serviced, maintained correctly and tested if necessary - with records to prove this.

If you are in an office this could be a printer or a laptop? Is it serviced and kept up to date with security, etc? Is it electrically tested? If the computer or laptop is important to your business then you may wish to consider keeping the item well looked after.

In a printing company, this will be machine maintenance, is it kept up to date, is preventative maintenance carried out? Is there a schedule?

In a car leasing company this could be the testing of motor vehicles to government standards, or servicing and preventive maintenance details. In a cleaning company it could be the personal protective equipment: is it safe, up to date and provided free of charge? In a building rental company it could be the testing of its building, its insurance policies, its gas and boiler testing.

I have given a flavour of what can be applied in any company giving a range of scenarios which includes, buildings, vehicles, tools and equipment, office equipment etc. This should give you a good idea of what applies in your organisation. What you need to ask yourself is what needs to be tested and what is important to your processes.

It may be a good idea to take a leaf out of ISO 27001 standard and make an asset register. The register could have details on where the asset is, when it is to be tested, whose responsibility it is and under what terms the servicing, maintenance or security features are kept up to date. You can have a few extra columns on an asset list indicating when servicing, calibration or testing is due? It's up to you but a great idea anyway, everything will be in one location and easy to find.

What you have to decide is which assets are most important in your company. What are the most important, at risk and valuable assets to you? If you can answer these few questions then you will be well on the way to deciding what the infrastructure is in your business and what it involves.

If in doubt always ask, please seek advice from those in the know: those who maintain and service, who are account holders or engineers. The equipment that you use may be subject to scrutiny; you should decide what applies to the necessities of your organisation. Something could be priceless to an organisation but only cost tens of pounds or dollars, assets should be controlled, they can also account for issues regarding losses, traceability and possible theft, which happens. So it also gives you a base for a yearly asset audit once or twice a year to help stop assets from 'floating' out of your doors.

When the auditor comes in, s/he will know your industry. Auditors are chosen with specific competence in a particular area, so if you are in engineering or software development (as an example), they'll know what to check and when to check it. They will look at your computers, check electrical servicing details, check security, make sure that maintenance is up to date and that software updates are kept on top of.

Be sure to keep track of what needs to be serviced, and when. This could save you some non- conformances and keep you firmly on track to achieve the standard.

Work environment

A lot can be said about work environments. The main point we should take into consideration when discussing your company is, are the areas to which the product or service is being undertaken suitable for that task?

If the areas involve people, are they warm enough? Is the atmosphere comfortable? Are they the correct size and are the facilities adequate for the purpose to which they are being used?

If you have controlled conditions, i.e. temperature and humidity in a testing laboratory, server room or engineering measuring department, these conditions and work environments are critical to the process.

This is where this clause is ideally suited. If you are measuring to microns or nanometres, you should not be carrying this out in a building where the temperature can alter coefficient of expansion properties of the materials. Testing should be carried out in controlled conditions, likewise any laboratory testing of certain materials or substances.

Work environments should also be conducive to the task: in other words the job should be carried out safely, professionally and precisely in an area that the employees are comfortable with.

The chances of non-conformance in an engineering workshop, office, retail outlet or design agency are very slim - unless you have everything piled high and wide and you cannot find anything when you may be under more scrutiny. However in fairness, this part of the standard does not really apply itself fully in most businesses because of the nature of the work.

I have given two examples of work environments that require controlling. If you think that you may have an issue on audit, seek advice and speak with your bosses.

Work environments are sometimes unavoidably unsuitable, because of funding or capacity maybe? It is how you utilise the work environment to your strengths is what matters.

You need to identify areas that may need a little more attention; however you are unlikely to fail an audit just for being a little messy or cluttered! It may not go down well and I for one like to see tidiness and structure, but we are not here to assess your cleanliness. It can be mentioned on audit but it would probably be an observation from the auditor – unless it was so bad that it would be raised as a non-conformance on clause 6.4. Having said that, when the auditor comes around to see your business, do your best to keep your work areas tidy and clean. This goes a long way to ensuring a smooth audit.

Work areas are also benches and desks, office spaces, computer server rooms. To enhance product conformity it helps to have clean desks and benches, free of mess and clutter.

If you were an engineer and you had lots of swarf (waste metal) lying around on a bench, then you went to measure a precision product that you had just machined, do you not think that you could damage or scratch your product? You could also damage the measuring equipment. Clean desks and areas help ensure that quality is maintained.

So work environment covers everything from buildings to workspaces, server rooms to car parks. Keep a look out for anywhere that may just compromise an audit because of mess or lack of good tradesmanship. And make sure you are on to anybody who falls foul of your good standards.

12.   Your services and products

Product realization is 7.0 in the standard.

Planning of product realization

"Planning of product realization" - this is a slightly strange term to describe the planning of your product or service. Remember earlier when I mentioned that the ISO has to translate into many different languages and can sound a bit strange to an English speaker? This is one such section.

Yes, the standard does sound confusing sometimes; but as I have previously suggested, it is for a purpose. Some say that the standards do not read well, my best advice is to take a look back and see your company through the eyes of each section of the standard. It is not just about interpretation of words; it is highly important that the interpretation of the necessary requirements revolves around your business.

Translated again it simply means how do you plan your product or service? Well only you should know that answer but put quite simply, do you apply the methodology or does your company just work it all out as you go along?

This clause means the planning of your product or service and how you go about it delivering it. In this clause you will see reference to clause 4.2.4 Control of records. Clearly, this means that you must be able to provide evidence of records to indicate that you have actually planned your projects, tasks, services and products.

Planning is one of the fundamental parts of excellent business practice. Without planning there is no format or structure, so even if you have a great product, if you fail to plan you are planning to fail.

This is a clause that can be excluded, as any can in section 7. However it is highly unlikely. Surely every company plans its operations, doesn't it? You would be surprised. It's a fact that all business do not plan for one matter or another, but in this day and age of business continuity plans and information security back up etc, the age of planning should be paramount.

No longer can you get away with knowing someone to get your foot in the door, no longer can businesses depend on locality and past exploits. Today's world is cut throat, even cynical; it is critical that planning and structure are part of your everyday routine. If you do not plan your products and services correctly then one day you will be found out and your company may be overlooked.

Planning your service is vital for three key business reasons: it helps your business to look organised and proper; it gives people and staff structure and guidance; and higher authorities look on you with greater appreciation and respect.

Let's consider planning of an important tender. What does the company putting a contract out to tender want? How is it to be processed? What are the timescales? Has the small print been read? Have you interpreted correctly what it is they are actually after? Do you have the manpower? All of these questions can be answered a lot quicker if your business already has information to hand.

Tenders and organisational background information are now looked into very seriously. Organisations are wary and will want you to prove yourselves, so they may want to know what structure and systems you have. You can be sure that 95 per cent of organisations or authorities putting work out to tender may, or will, request that you have a system or maybe formal accreditation such as ISO 9001 (Quality) / ISO 14001 (Environmental) / BS OHSAS 18001 (Occupational health and safety) / ISO 27001 (Information Security) / BS 25999 (Business Continuity) etc – or maybe even more, or, at the least a management structure in these areas.

ISO 9001 can be worth up to five per cent of a tender, itself not to be sniffed at if the tender is worth half a million pounds or more. But if the company that you are up against for the contract plans well and has formal accreditation in place while your similarly qualified company lacks those things, who is going to win the business? Planning is everything, and its importance runs from the top to the bottom of your organisation.

So what are you to do about it if your company is in the no-planning boat? First, map out what it is your business is trying to achieve. What are you trying to complete or manufacture? What has to happen before product commencement can begin and flourish? What materials and products does your business require to get going? What training and experience are required from your staff? Are there certain types of tools and equipment that they or you need?

What about when they are trained correctly? What is the process for them to follow? Do you have guidelines? This is all very relevant and depending upon the size of the business the amount of procedures can differ. Do not fall into the trap of people telling you that the important stuff is in their heads; map it out and plan it with them if you have to.

Do meetings have to be planned so that your customers are kept well informed if necessary? What legal responsibilities do you have as a business that you need to conform to? Does the customer place any extra responsibility on you with requirements that are not legally binding with UK regulation but binding in a contract (therefore legally binding) with you?

There are many realms in which this sphere of planning can make itself apparent.

The first thing you need to identify is who does your business plans? What is involved and who is involved? Do your personnel plan to fine detail – depending on what needs to be planned?

All these questions are designed to make you think about your business and view it in the light that I would when auditing or consulting. What is it that your business needs to do in the planning stakes? Who is involved, and is that process worth mapping out? The answer to that is 'yes'. Business planning requires thorough mapping. The ISO/certificating body will only let you have a certificate if you plan correctly.

You have to decide what needs to be mapped and how to do it. One of the modern approaches is doing it by flowchart, using software like Microsoft Visio or something similar.

Many organisations like to have a 'quality plan'. That is a way of planning each stage of a product or service, and may involve the important factors when planning your product right through to the completion stage. They can be as in-depth or as easy as you want.

If I was auditing your company, I would look at your product or service and decide how in depth it was. Then if I recognised that you needed more planning I would say so and recommend further action.

The standard asks for six mandatory procedures; but it also says that you should map out your important processes in a way that is identifiable, pertinent and necessary. There is nothing worse than going into a company with six mandatory procedures of about a page each and a quality manual that is five pages long. That may suffice if you are not doing much at all, but in a larger and more complex environment, more planning is necessary.

This is because people like to know what they should be doing. They like to reference information now and again and to check if they are doing things correctly. So please map your planning processes out to whatever it is that your company does.

Customer-related processes

Determination of requirements related to the product

Determination of requirements related to the product means that you must listen to how the customer wants the product or service delivered.

Obviously, this area is so vast and changeable to each business that, like most of the clauses in 7, each company will differ for this part of the standard.

Determining the requirements is something that you can do only by speaking to your customers and your people. Let me give a few examples. If you worked in the pharmaceutical industry, the specification of ingredients for manufacture must be followed to the letter to avoid the possibility of prosecution should something go wrong?

Or take the case of a nuclear reactor. The classification, grade, content and physical properties of a piece of weapons grade uranium are essential factors to get right. The stringency of these must be astronomical: but somewhere along the process, somebody or a group of professionals would have put their heads together and worked out exactly what the customer wants, and determining that, is crucial.

So what is the best thing to do? First, ask your customers and clients what they need, want and expect. If you can deliver these things, you should have a great relationship with your customers.

Of course there may be a situation where your company feels that you must also determine your own requirements of the product that the purchaser may not ask for. You would do this to give a purchaser extra confidence in your abilities or to demonstrate that you are taking effective care over your products.

One area of this part of the standard is regulations, either statutory or given codes of practice that your customer (or you) may want to include in the determining of your products to ensure greater quality and efficiencies.

Codes of practices come in many forms, such as BS 8900 which applies to sustainability management. Some standards are not necessarily auditable however; and codes of practice and recognised best forms of practice are available for many products and services.

Codes of practices, standards, laws and guidelines are available for you to get your product right. Your customer may not always impress this upon you; but this is an area that you may want to research and explore, especially if you are in the safety industry and are providing equipment to people whose welfare may depend on it.

There are many other business and sectors that require correct standardisation and codes of practice. You will have to look these up for your sector, and doing so may help you add further value to your business.

The customer will need to feel confident that the delivery and post delivery activities are in place and structured to provide an effective facilitation of the product from your site to theirs. They may want detailed deliveries and planning times set around *their* customers' requirements, so timely delivery may be essential.

You could have the finest product in the world but if it is late, your customer may still frown upon you. Ever missed some important post because it was mailed late? Have you ever gone to a shop only to be told that your dream product can't be delivered for two weeks?

Delivering correctly and on time will help you retain your customers. Also, if problems ever arise, effective planning increases the time for problem solving.

Your organisation may also want to consider maintenance contracts or extra provisions after a product or service has been delivered. The customer may require follow-up support and a guidance booklet. All this detail helps you to determine the customer's requirements.

There may also be contractual situations that can lead to disputes. It's therefore even more important to get these requirements right because not doing so can prove costly.

If you are arranging an agreement with a client, get it written down and accepted before progressing. When consulting I always write out an order acknowledgement and terms and conditions so my clients know exactly what they are getting. It corresponds directly with our quote and the detail is taken exactly as written from there so there is no ambiguity or argument. I do this because (a) it tells them what I am going to do, (b) when I am going to do it and in what timeframe and (c) what the terms and conditions of the agreement are.

In this case when determination of customer requirement is sometimes accepted just before delivery, you have to be prepared to walk away if they do not accept your terms right at the closure. You could send these terms two weeks prior to your first visit of course, and from a professional point of view this customer determination should already be accepted before I walk through the door. A detailed quote must be accepted and a purchase order of the requested services should be mandatory for any business. Do not proceed with your service until you have full acceptance and the customer is happy with what you are providing. Determination is absolutely critical.

If the customer says to me that he is not happy, I only have to point out the identity of the quote and the order acknowledgement. This rarely happens however because I go out of my way to make sure that the customer is pleased.

Try to keep out of trouble with them though, remember, your customer pays you, best to keep them on the right side and treat them as you would like to be treated yourself. If you plan properly, you keep the customer in the loop and you cross all legal and regulatory points, you will be fine. If not, be ready for trouble.

Review of requirements related to the product

This clause is very similar to the previous one. The review of a requirement differs slightly however because the perspective is placed on checking after the planning of your product rather than just planning.

It has everything to do with the planning stage and is conducted before any product is supplied.

So what does this mean for your industry? As always this is bespoke for each and every sector so I will give you examples of what to check for.

Your product, whatever it may entail, needs checking and the main purpose of a quality system is that matters are reviewed, the customer is kept in the loop and you can demonstrate effective product or service review before a product is made or delivered.

If you were manufacturing a car, it would be best to validate any requirements before the purchasing begins. This is because you want to get the planning detail correct before you start to progress further with the order.

Defining product and service requirements and getting the customer to agree to them are paramount. It may save you time and face should something go wrong that you have not planned, agreed and reviewed with the client.

This is a crucial area. As explained in the previous clause, possible prosecution could occur if you have not consulted with the client fully and kept them in full conversation with your planning and detail.

Let us say that you were to change certain requirements at the last stage of planning before manufacture and you decided that the client would not need to know because in your eyes the detail is only minor.

Taking a fictitious example of a bolt for an aircraft fuselage, the client wants the length of the bolt to be 38.50 mm and you can only get 38.40 mm for whatever reason. You decide not to tell them because it is only 0.1 of a millimetre and who is going to find out anyway – and would it even matter?

So you deliver the goods and the client is happy – until they find out that the bolt is under tolerance by 0.1 mm. Before making this discovery, they have fastened 48 wings to fuselages with the bolts.

The clients realise that the reduced length will cause the torque rating to become inaccurate because the bolt cannot reach far enough in its housing to correctly seat the wings, therefore leading to a loss of applied pressure on the wing joints. They check all of the bolts and find that you have manufactured a consistently imperfect product. They then call your Managing Director and inform him that they have just wrongly assembled 24 aircraft, that are due for delivery to Bqmc co uk Airlines in a week – and it is your company's fault because they gave you the criteria and you did not apply it correctly.

It is unlikely that your firm would win the inevitable legal battle that would follow. The results could be calamitous, perhaps involving your company going out of business.

This is a fictitious story and a worst-case scenario, but stranger things have happened. Something similar could happen to you if you do not meet customer requirements. So whatever is involved with your product or service, be sure to provide your customer with all the details and get them to accept the criteria in a contract. Especially if the requirements of the product change part way through, because you cannot manufacture something perfectly?

Hopefully you can see that a review of requirements is something you cannot afford to miss. At the planning and designing stages, these areas of business require you to be on the ball.

If the customer does not provide you with detail, it is up to your company to do it. You must provide the detail for them and get acceptance for it. I have seen problems with many companies when they are carrying out work that is not accepted before processing.

In one case, I knew of some work being started and completed without full authorisation. Tens of thousands of pounds worth of work came under scrutiny because the director failed to get a customer acceptance and review of what was happening. Large scale indeed.

If your client is unwilling to put pen to paper to accept what you are making or the service you are providing, you need to be wary. This requirement is part of an international standard for two parties' benefits. Yours, to protect you from issues, time wasted, possible financial waste or heavy fines leading to possible business loss; your customer's, to save them from possibly defective parts and a ruined reputation.

The answer is a simple one: get the acceptance from your customer. If you change the requirements or detail, get further acceptance for the amendments from the highest authority in that organisation that you need for a 'go / no go answer'.

I once helped an organisation that changed drawings when it felt like it to suit their design and build. When I came to internally audit them I asked to see client authorisation for the amendments, and the person in charge could not give them to me. There were no formal acceptances.

Get the process or product reviewed and bring in other people to help you. Get client authorisation for the product requirements and amendments and make sure it is legally bound. Or stand by for the consequences if something goes wrong. Your directors need to be fully aware of this clause: but this area is especially crucial, ISO standard or not.

Customer communication

Customer communication is a delightful part of this standard because it forces companies to speak to their customers. Because believe it or not, some organisations do not want to.

What should be included to pass this part of the standard? The main focus when auditing is on the customer communication lines, are they intact and working? Is there any feedback, speaking to your customers about your delivered services and after sales. This is the purchaser's chance of telling you just how good (or bad) they think your product is. This is discussed in 8.2.1 as well.

How should you go about discussing matters with them? Email and telephone are probably the two appropriate, with the former providing good records. There are a number of ways to ascertain satisfaction. One of the best is of course the customer questionnaire, but this can be ineffective if you just email it or post it to them without follow up. In my experience you should get your questionnaire up on screen and telephone them to get some real input.

Then, go through the questions when it is convenient. You must tell them that it will take up only two or three minutes of their precious time, remember that some people really do not want to be bothered with this kind of approach. If you target 50, you may get 25 good quality pieces of feedback. What should you be asking them?

First of all your questions can be set out from 1 - 5 and some examples for you to choose are as follows:

(1) Is the product or service working correctly and to your satisfaction?

(2) Is there anything that you would wish to see done better?

(3) Is there any part of our product / service that you think is of paramount importance?

4) Is there an addition that you would like to see?

5) Would you be interested in any of our other products?

6) What makes you want to fill in a company questionnaire? (This one is tongue in cheek; but you will be surprised at some honest answers that may help you to be more efficient in the future.)

Of course, there are many other possible questions, and feel free to devise your own as long as they are bespoke to your business. This approach is successful because you are giving value to the person's input. Make them feel special if you can.

Other ways to do this are a scoring system based on a set of thought-out questions; this can help to improve quality performance. If you ask for scores and you would like an average score of 75 per cent (and you get 70 per cent), you can ask your customers what they would like to see as an improvement in your product or service. People's feedback can be really important, especially if you are giving the user a valued experience. It can actually help to boost your profits if you listen; but the question is, do you want to ask?

You can put the increased target on your quality policy and make it a company goal. How are you going to increase your customer experience, how can you improve? All exciting stuff when you get involved, this is really an area where quality control can help you to push the boundaries of your business. Seek and you will find, as the saying goes.

I have come across a few organisations that do not want to speak to their potential customers, even when they have just lost a multi-million pound contract to a competitor. I ask them if they have spoken to them about it, they say no. If you do not ask where you are going wrong, how will you avoid making the same mistakes again?

You need to push people to give you answers, as I have described in previous chapters. Other people's advice and input can only be encouraging, especially if you are losing business. You must ask what you can do better. Don't be put off by reluctance on their part; if you put in a tender or a proposal, the least someone can do is to give you some feedback on your efforts.

One of the parts of this section is what to do if a customer complains. This must be recorded and kept a record of, corrective and preventive actions must be put into place to check that matters have been resolved and customer dialogue must be present in some form.

If this complaint is formal, I would expect a formal resolution, a paper trail of information relating to the issue, director input and a response from the complainant. For some companies this paper trail may be one piece, or, in the case of a large-scale business such as an airline manufacturer the detail may cover thousands, depending on the criticality.

What you must do is make sure that the complaint is taken seriously and followed up. I think it highly important that you have a procedure and / or a separate recording form for this area. It is standard good practice to record complaints on their own forms.

You must put corrective actions into place after a complaint and you must resolve the issue if you want to get or keep your ISO certificate. It isn't good enough to just shrug your shoulders and say that "they are always complaining".

Take the case of one fictitious organisation selling goods. I ask to see their customer complaints and they tell me they have none. I ask for their returned goods records in the past six months – and find that 52 goods were returned. To delve further, I would ask what the returns comments are and why the customers are asking for a refund their money. If the reasons were varied, I would need to go into further detail to find out causes etc. That is what you should do. If you are selling items and people are returning them, record the comments and find out what is going wrong. This will improve your awareness and maybe you can fix the issues, reducing the number of unhappy customers. But it's all about listening to those customers in the first place and assessing any possible trends.

Other information that would be sought to justify passing this part of the standard includes product information, enquiries, amendments and contracts. If you satisfy the previous three clauses then this should be no problem. Remember, some of your processes will cover more than one part of the standard.

Product information should be given to the purchaser though, which is one area that I have not previously covered. Product information again varies per sector. If it was a DVD manufacturer, then how to work the DVD information is a must – even if men do not read instructions! For safety clothing or safety footwear it would be a good idea to give product information, state how mush pressure a boot may take, where it should be used and what not to do, i.e. how to not compromise the workwear. If you are making children's climbing frames then you should give detailed assembly advice and safety information.

It all differs as to what your business does; just make sure to give detailed information to your customers and get feedback on your services and products.

Design and development

Design and development is a very detailed part of the standard and you tend to find some companies trying to avoid including it.

There are many cases of companies saying that they wish to exclude this clause when it is clearly evident that they cannot. Here are a few questions that might help clarify this part of the standard:

Do you design and develop your products?

Do you carry out design (or further design) on initial customer supplied drawings?

Do you design any of your products, no matter how small or how unimportant to you?

Do you design any drawing / product / service for any other third party that they pay you for and use in business?

If you have answered yes to any of the above questions then you should not be excluding this because the simple matter is that you 'design' in some capacity – which is enough for me and my fellow auditors.

When discussing parts of section 7, look at the standard, look at your company and then decide. There are cases when organisations may try to exclude a clause because they know that if they don't, it may cause them a few difficulties. Why? The reason is because a few organisations do not carry out this function with enough detail, do not provide enough trained/experienced personnel and give little serious thought to clarifying and verifying the designs with the customer. As I said before, if you do not get your designs accepted and you press on without customer say-so or written authority, you may be heading for an issue somewhere along the line.

Design is such a crucial aspect of businesses that many organisations feel that they must be highly professional, technically proficient and detailed with their planning. Organisations that fall into these categories are amongst some of the finest in the world.

Design is crucial because most of what we do or use is designed to a very high specification. If you look at Apple computers for instance, they are designed to perfection (or near perfection), so advanced, robust and solidly built that those who use Apple computers, swear that they are the finest material thing that they own. Or you could take a Rolls Royce, an Aston Martin, a Typhoon (Euro fighter): all highly capable machines that are seriously built and designed to the very highest of standards and specifications.

Before they are built, they are designed with the finest intention and those that design them are hand-picked craftsmen at the summit of their profession.

Obviously we cannot all afford some prices of motor, aircraft or information technology engineering so we buy other products that are excellent value for the money that we pay for them. For some, these may still be the pinnacle even if they can afford more, it is your own personal choice which counts.

There are many examples of such high quality products and services, Microsoft software, Lexus cars, Dell computers, BMW, Audi, I could go on and on about such well designed machines and software to go with them. To be honest, opinions about products matter to only one person – yourself. You may like or dislike those I have mentioned; but these designs have stood the test of time and are excellent value. My point is that if you design your products and services like the previously mentioned, the chances are that you will shine through any tough economic times, even a recession.

The other point of this is, if you are considering excluding design, the auditors will not get a chance to audit it and help you along the way. Of course, an auditor is not supposed to give consultancy but they may help you to weed out problems and situations. After all, an auditor is not there to bring you down, he is there to help to bring value to your company by auditing you to a national or international standard.

Most auditors are very experienced in their fields. They will bring value but you must listen. As I always say, those who don't listen to professional people that can help are weaker than those who do. Taking such advice is a strength, not a weakness.

Design and development planning

Planning is major area – and the design of the planning stages is almost as important as the design itself!

Planning can be carried out at your organisation in a number of ways, by meetings (minuted for records), emails, letters, designs, correspondence, faxes, design software and pretty much anything else. Planning is also vitally important for the customer. Does it fit, is it going into another product that is being made elsewhere (apart from the customers premises)? Remember that you may be designing your product with one customer or more in mind. But let's say that the customer is having all of their products designed and made by other companies and they only fit them together at their premises. Who do you think you should be planning with then? Correct, both companies; and if there is a third or fourth company involved, you should speak with them as well.

A customer will give you planning tolerances if they have any worth, because tolerances give you a margin of error or improvement. When you are planning you need to know these matters and write them down.

You need to know scales, projections (third / first angle), tolerances, materials used, grades, priorities, timescales, non conformity reporting, testing, checking for problems, authority for design, capability of the person designing, communication lines and outputs, development stages. Is it done in stages or periods throughout the year, or do they want it all in one go? Dimensional accuracy and standardisation is to be thought through (make sure if your customer wants millimetres you are not designing in centimetres)! You may laugh, but some organisations / individuals in companies may do this. Get the detail correct and you will be fine.

Who is verifying the product? Who is validating the designs and who gives the authority to proceed or not? Who needs to be part of the interfacing of the designs, who else is involved? Where are they based? Who is noting amendments and getting client authority to proceed?

All of this is relevant. Now you can see why some organisations shriek at this clause. Don't be scared; if you design, get stuck in and get it right! Good design gives a product strength and durability, if your products are well designed, it is a good bet that your customers will think a great deal more of you.

There may be many more items to the previous list, I have just given you a handful of matters to think about and should help you to shine some light on this subject if you are in the dark about what to do.

Design and development inputs

Inputs are the building blocks to designing. The inputs will determine your outputs and, of course, how good your product is.

A product that has had excellent input is likely to excel; a product lacking input and thought is less likely to do so.

The auditor will review what your inputs are and check that the customer is kept fully involved throughout the entire design process if necessary. Communication is a great part of this clause, although it is not mentioned as much as I would like to see in the standard. The specifics and depth of communication will vary according to your product. If an auditor suspects that you are lacking in communication, they may raise a concern. I certainly would if I suspected that your customers were kept out of the design loop.

Inputs can come from many angles. They will include staff involvement and depth of inputs, functional requirements of what it is that you are designing. If there is any legal compliance to go with the product, that will need to be taken into consideration. Maybe your company places extra requirements on the product, or your customers want you to have extra requirements. These could also involve a national or international standard as I have mentioned in previous chapters.

It may also be necessary to take your designs from sources that have been proved in other areas; for instance, you may be adapting a product for use that has been derived from another source or company. If this is so, have you got the authorisation to use someone else's designs? If you are using other people's designs, make sure you have written and legal authority.

You may also have designs that you are building on that are your or your organisation's technical property. If so, do you have the authority to proceed from your peers and anyone at a higher level who needs to be involved?

The planning of a product must be well recorded where appropriate and you should have records indicating the various stages of development. The technical aspect of the product will depend on the depth of detail. Designing a new piece of pipe will require less input than an electronic circuit board for a satellite. Each input has to be commensurate with the level of complication that the item or service requires.

Also, designs should not be in conflict with other designs. If you are designing equipment to fit into someone else's equipment, it is vitally important that there is compatibility and accuracy of tolerance.

These inputs are high on the importance scale. Proper fits, and limits to those fits, have to be highly accurate. The standard ISO 286-2:2010 Geometrical product specifications (GPS) is the ISO code system for tolerances on linear sizes. You may need to take advantage of such international standards on a range of practical applications.

The other point to make is that you don't want your designs to be ambiguous. The greater the degree of flexibility in a design, the greater the chance of complications further down the design route. An ambiguous design may cast doubt on the ability to manufacture it correctly.

When a design is planned, it can sometimes take another form when manufactured because of materials and material properties etc. A great deal of planning input will be directed to your choice of material. In the case of metals, carbon content and additions of other alloys can cause properties in a material that are wholly inconsistent with your product. If you are designing with plastics, monomers and polymers must be considered. The characteristics that may be displayed on manufacture could be totally out of synchronisation with what you are expecting. We will speak more about design validation later in clause 7.

The greatest input and building block of your designs however is the one I mentioned at the very start of this clause: your staff, and how well educated and trained they are. Experience in designing is one area of input that you cannot overlook or cut corners on, especially with staff.

Design and development outputs

An output is measured by your product. A design can only be truly tested when it has been put to the test operationally. This clause *is* your business, it is everything, it is what makes your business tick over; because without output, there is no business.

Outputs on a design vary, but this part of the standard is helping you to ensure that variations in outputs are stamped out as much as possible unless you have an open approach and agreement with your customers. The outputs are covered in the following parts of clause 7.3 too. Outputs come in the form of verification (of design and product – is it correct?), validation (does it work?), review (stages of design and check points) and changes (what happens when amendments are carried out?).

The output of design should match the criteria supplied by your customers: because if it does not, have you the authority to make a concession with them? As I described with the fabricated airline situation, if you change the inputs, the outputs may change too and customers need to know. The auditor will be looking for these changes, and will check that what is going in is coming out, as it were.

Output will also cover the approval of your outputs. Is approval necessary before full production begins? Do you need written authority to proceed? All this is vital. Many a company has proceeded without full acceptance and a verified design. Organisations can be so focused on sales, profits and growth that they sometimes forget to ask for final design approval. The easy answer is write a procedure explaining that output is to be fully discussed with the customer with full consent and approval before a galaxy of produce is manufactured. If the customer does not approve and you make tens, hundreds, thousands or even millions of products without their say so, the business could go bankrupt if the customer does not want them.

I hope that you can now see the benefits of applying an international standard properly. By 'properly', I mean, fully integrating the standard into your organisation and its operations.

The outputs must meet and match full design criteria for development and match that of the previously described inputs. The outputs must match up with the purchasing requirements and they must contain reference criteria where appropriate.

One of the important outputs is the criteria specified for safe and proper use. Instructions must be designed too for this application; because if you do not tell someone how to work a product or provide safety information, then you are wide open for reprisals. Safety information should cover as much as possible, starting with the usual: electrical, mechanical and operating instructions, what not to do and information on products that may cause health and safety issues when used improperly.

There will be many issues of health, safety, operational and product information. You just have to decide on what they are for your organisation's product or service and get them to the user.

Design and development review

A review is a natural development in assessing design management. After all, would you allow someone to just design a product and allow it through the door without a second glance from someone else in your company? Of course not, you say; but it has been known to happen.

If you are allowing someone to design your products without a review or a check from someone else in your organisation, then think again. This is unwise, for a number of reasons. Even the most skilled design engineer can be influenced by factors such as tiredness, stress, family issues, other work concerns, pressures and commitments, boss issues, health problems or even eyesight difficulties. People don't just bring their lunch and sandwiches to work!

You never know what may be affecting someone: and if that someone designs your products without even the most cursory of checks, this is asking for trouble. Have it checked, by a member of staff qualified to do so. This is a vital safeguard for your company.

The standard asks for suitable stages of review. That really is dependent on your product and how important it is viewed by you and by your customers. I cannot tell you what the suitable stages are; you must cast a professional eye on your design requirements and decide with your staff what the timeframe for checking is. One important question is? Do you carry out a full check at each stage of the design? If there is a systematic staged design requirement, it may be prudent to carry out a full review of the design and send it to the customer for approval at each stage.

The customer should be kept fully involved in a design process and be engaged with the criteria for fulfilment of acceptance. In my view, the customer should give full acceptance and authority to proceed at every stage (if feasible). The written acceptance of a design is crucial and paramount if you want to protect your company from potential repercussions: and you should get acceptance in writing from the highest authority in the customer's company, if possible.

The main purpose of a review is obviously to check, but also to identify any potential problems, issues and necessary actions that may have been overlooked or are required.

The review must evaluate any potential issues for the ability of the design to meet the criteria when manufactured. There may be issues when the design has been manufactured for the first time and a validatory requirement may be needed before full production can commence. As I have explained previously, this is another area of design that must not be overlooked. I will discuss this in more detail in clause 7.3.6.

The review(s) should ideally be minuted and records be available for the auditors to check. It is a mandatory requirement that you shall have records; if you check this part of the standard it will tell you that records must be available. Most organisations I come across do not have great records for discussing issues and reviews on design, please try and get something written down for the sake of your business if not the standard, it may be crucial if there are any disputes?

When the international standard identifies that records are to be made available it will tell you so, usually mentioning clause 4.2.4 which is control of records.

Reviews should consist of personnel that have important input in the designing process. This differs between companies, but the main people you should consider are a designer (or more than one, depending on the product and difficulty of design), a company director, engineers as appropriate, possibly one or more customer representatives, operators with experience of such equipment or services, and anybody that you deem important for ensuring that your designs are assessed and evaluated.

If you are a one-man operation, get a secondary opinion from an external and unaffiliated professional that will discuss this matter with you in an honest and open way. I would want to pay someone that will say to me that this may not work, or that something is not right.

On audit, a lot of issues come with design reviews not being properly carried out or glossed over by the organisation. Reviews are necessary because they protect your company from issues with your customers.

Standards have these clauses included for a very good reason: the detail that they require you to have is very well proven and documented because they have helped many a business to succeed. Role model businesses have ensured that fundamental pieces of standards are followed and included, which is why they are in the standard.

That is why when the United Nations is helping to build economies, it relies on proven national and international standards to help upcoming organisations to grow. When someone shuns a standard or even a clause, remind them of this fact.

Design and development verification

Verification, or verifying, is a clause that ties in well with the previous clause of review. This is because you are reviewing and verifying at the same time, in conjunction with your staff. So records of review and acceptance of review can also help with the records of verification. When you verify a design and accept it, that is a review nonetheless and is an easy way of covering this clause of the standard.

Verifying should be performed at planned arrangements. The review does what it says and the verification aspects can come at a time when the reviews are accepted and the go-ahead is given by either the organisation or the customer.

Customer verification is central to your design activities, and a verification of acceptance of design should be in evidence. These chief aspects will cover an organisation should any difficulties or issues arise.

The fundamental part of verification is to check that all inputs and outputs correspond with each other and that the client's requirements have been fully met.

Should the customer wish to review and verify your input and outputs in the design process, you will have no trouble satisfying them if the records are present.

That is a main part that the auditor will be checking for. The auditor seeks approval from your design process: and more importantly, from your customers.

When auditors come to visit you and you know that some aspects may not be in place, it is far better to be honest and own up to any shortcomings. This is because the auditor will possibly look on you with a favourable eye, rather than find something that you tried to hide or exclude without proper authority.

You have to remember that if the auditor is acting on behalf of two bodies, i.e. the certification body and a national accreditation body. You have to justify to them that you are capable of meeting the standards you are being audited against.

If the auditor feels that there may be important aspects missing in your design process then they may be less likely to give approval for certification, because the final say rests with a certification committee. I would certainly not sanction a certificate had I felt that a company were missing vital aspects of design that might possibly be compromised and result in a safety failure. I have done it before and would do so again, as an auditor you are there to audit / sanction a process when sampling the evidence, so if, in the future that process comes under legal scrutiny, you may be asked to give evidence.

If I am acting on behalf of an organisation and the person being audited is not conforming to requirements and I feel that health and safety or product integrity is being compromised, then I would not pass them on audit. If they corrected that matter, then there would be reconsideration on appropriate checking.

Verification arrangements shall be in place and a record of it will be in evidence and maintained.

Design and development validation

Validation is a similar sounding clause to the previous one, and people can often make a mistake when implementing this part of the standard.

To highlight the difference and to put it into more understandable terms, let's take the example of a motor car manufacturer. Would it just design its cars and start producing them without testing them beforehand? Hardly. The manufacturer will put the car through a series of electronic and mechanical tests to validate that its safety, mechanical and electrical performance meets the required standards before production gets under way. This rigorous testing will be fundamental to its success, both in finding errors and pinpointing strengths.

Maybe you will need to test your product in a variety of environments, applying high pressures, temperatures or other forces? Trying to test or maybe even 'break' your product could give you an edge over your competitors, if you can identify those weaknesses via a validation process, you can increase your product quality by knowing how to stop problems occurring.

If a manufacturer did not complete a design check, faults could possibly be missed that may be potentially serious. If the cars were built without sufficient checks, the errors would still come to light – but they would be found by the users, with possibly deadly results. In today's world, this is an area manufacturers cannot overlook.

If you have a design department, what do you think will be your approach of validating a design and checking that it works properly? If you manufacture, maybe you need test pieces and also other items that the manufactured part may need to be fitted into or bolted together.

When a validation is carried out, sometimes a mock-up of what you are fitting it to may need to be constructed? Where I have previously worked, we manufactured process trays that fitted inside oil refinery columns. The mock-up of the column was completed in the workshop and the trays were assembled inside the mock-up diameter of the column, to ensure that the design fitted after manufacture, simple but highly effective.

Of course, some designs cannot be validated until after manufacture, or until they reach the end user. In such cases, it is wise to adapt your processes to suit and ensure that your design process is strengthened by applying other factors to minimise any issues that may arise.

You could have checks from another draughtsman, checks when you are manufacturing other parts that fit together. A way of validating the design can be sought but it is occasionally necessary to wait for the end user to validate the work by actually using it. As a consultancy in assisting companies to achieve these standards, we may not validate the systems we have inserted and helped to build, it is the certification bodies that provide a validation service for companies such as bqmc, because ultimately, they validate the system and check (via their service) if our work is up to the standard and give our customers a certificate.

Validating a design should take place before delivery but there are occasions where it is just not possible, so you must decide the path for your business – or exclude it from your scope of business on accreditation. Either way, your responsibility is unavoidable and design validation is still of high importance to the end user whichever way you look upon it.

As usual, records shall be required to authenticate your validation process.

Control of design and development changes

Controlling changes and amendments to design are a key to the final acceptance criteria. This is because when a design has been changed to suit alterations and modifications, the changes must be recorded and kept under scrutiny for customer acceptance.

When a design is under commencement, occasionally there are required changes that it will be necessary to record. However, any change to a design should be recorded no matter how small the detail. That's because, if you are changing any design to suit differing technical outputs, you need to keep your customer abreast of all alterations to any part of the original structure or agreed specification. As we have talked about previously, when changes are made, if they are not authorised, this can sometimes jeopardise the final product. Any change should be the subject of recorded discussion and debate, any alteration should be classified with a high value so that everyone is involved who needs to be.

When you alter a design, you should record the details in at least two places on the drawing. One in the title block or information area on the drawing itself, the second a note on the design near to the modification with a line and arrow pointing toward it. This is good drawing and technical best practice. It is also advisable to have a modifications log as separate.

Then the design team or head of design should be consulted, followed by a director. If approved by your organisation, your customer should also be consulted and possibly give the final say on such a matter.

This might not be the exact route that all designs follow in all organisations. Sometimes special jurisdiction and dispensation can be given to a design team and the legal responsibility may be placed on them to perform. But it is vital for you to inform the customer anyway, just to be sure – even if they just tell you to get on with it.

Design amendments should also carry a revision. If an initial start drawing is revision 0 (zero) and then if you make a change, the next could be 1, 2, 3... *or* A, B, C... and so on. Each time, I personally would expect the customer to authenticate and accept the design – in writing or at the very least by signed email, fax, PDF or some similar format.

These changes shall be reviewed properly, with appropriate input from other members where required, and there shall be an evaluation as to how the design will be affected.

All designs and changes should consist of well kept records and detailed record keeping. If you are designing and making changes, I would monitor and record all changes and keep the records in two places, in a file on a computer and a hard copy at least.

Keep changes recorded and detailed where they need to be. The worst thing that can happen on audit is that changes and amendments on the factory or workshop do not reflect those in the design offices.

What I usually do when auditing is take a sample of five or six drawings and then go to the manufacturing area and check to see if they have the same revision that they are working on, or get drawings from the workshop and check with the design office.

Occasionally, designers do not pass on the changed designs where appropriate after a revision has been produced. This can lead to masses of trouble – especially if left unchecked.

If changes are left un-scrutinised and uncontrolled, eventually the product could end up in the customer's premises with incorrect revisions of the design. In other words, the customer will be expecting a higher revision of product than you have designed. To combat this, the design office and the workshop must communicate effectively. Even a team of designers operating half a world away must have a good rapport and communication line with the staff who are manufacturing the product. This must be by appropriate communication. And, on audit, you must prove that the appropriate communication is more than satisfactory.

It is useful to have opening meetings in the morning or at shift changes, where amendments and issues are discussed between parties. These provide an excellent forum for controlling change.

Purchasing

Purchasing process

I once went into a business to assist them. This business had been trading for many years. On my first day I asked to see how they purchased their supplies; they said that they picked up the telephone and ordered them. I then asked where they recorded this information, and was told that they didn't. After XX number of years, I felt that it was time for a change!

Not every business has a hold of its own procedures. If you cannot control your expenditure, what chance do you have of succeeding? Not much, I would say.

When I look at an international standard and its clauses, I know that they are there for a reason. Remember, if standards are good enough for hundreds of thousands of other organisations, they are good enough for most of us.

With the advent of information technology and excellent accounting packages, this part of the standard has become increasingly well controlled from a purchasing controller's point of view, it is certainly showing on audit.

The purchasing process is becoming increasingly streamlined and accurate with modern purchasing information technology like the Sage package. This allows you to control suppliers, products, prices, accounts, purchases, purchase order numbers and delivery notes etc. It does everything – when used correctly and to the full.

These systems are highly accurate. The only one thing that causes problems is an error in input. The sheer processing ability of some software packages is reducing the size of purchasing departments. I once worked at a factory and the purchasing department was almost as big as the engineering block. The factory housed 3000 personnel so you can imagine the purchases involved. Today, the advent of such great computing power has reduced numbers quite significantly.

However for the rest of us who cannot get purchasing software or may not even need it, we have to do it another way. The main aspect in purchasing is controlling what you buy and having reference numbers and purchase orders etc. Purchase orders are increasingly common and have become like a receipt of a purchase for the supplier. Most suppliers will ask for a purchase order receipt because they like to think that it validates the purchase and the customer is less likely to cancel the order.

A purchase number system is easy to set up. You can start at whatever you want to, maybe add your company initials if you so wish but this is not necessary, just ensure that you understand it, personally I just started at '1'. You can easily set up a purchasing database on Microsoft excel or open office documents, which is easy to learn and effective if you have a small team that requires quick logging of purchases.

Of course purchasing should be well controlled, and the bigger the business the more complex the system; but with the arrival of these purchasing functions, you should need not worry too much about your references etc. What you should do is log your purchases, no matter what the medium and where the purchase has been purchased for a contract or a specific reason, it is wise to reference that contract as well on the paperwork

I'm often asked, "What if we buy in bulk for more than one contract?" The answer is straightforward: as long as you have a purchase reference for the goods you can allocate the amounts to certain contracts, as long as this is within reason and relates to your references.

If you buy 10,000 nuts and bolts, they would just be marked for stock. If the purchase is more complicated, such as buying 100 hard drives for your computer building business, you may want to include information on the build paperwork by using serial numbers or identifications where possible. Use common sense and don't overcomplicate the standard or your approach, the more numbers that are involved, the chances for errors are increased.

These methods, although well defined, can have many different routes. If an auditor is asking you why you didn't reference your 10,000 nuts and bolts, he may be being pedantic; unless you are building an aircraft, space shuttle or something highly sophisticated and safety driven. I always insist on the method suiting the task or contract.

Purchasing should be well controlled. In the businesses that I see, someone is usually in complete control of it and I rarely find problems. The issues usually come in a business where the purchase comes into the premises and it is incorrectly built, the wrong parts are sent, there is not enough or there is too much, and so on. We shall cover this matter in 7.4.3.

Suppliers

Suppliers should be monitored and checked upon, depending on the importance of their delivered product.

We must apply some common sense, however. If we just buy office goods from the best shop, this should be explained carefully to the auditor – and this will be understood if this is all that you do. It is still a good idea to reference your purchase orders to the product of course. If you are buying online, maybe it is because of a recommendation, you have used them before and are happy with their produce, all good reasons to buy, so explain why you do to the auditor.

Suppliers will be evaluated depending on the criteria that you yourself will specify. The specification can depend on how you view the importance of your activities and the impact that incorrect products can have on your organisation and your business output.

Many companies that I visit have a structure in place and a simple scoring system, which is usually all that is needed. Usually a quality or business management system is one area that scores highly, as this will show that the supplier in question may have a degree of quality in their approach.

You should be aware however, that some companies with a quality management system do not protect the quality of their products and supplies enough. That may be due to their quality system not being properly integrated into the business? That company may just want a certificate for marketing purposes and may not be that serious about it on the inside. Another reason could be that the company does not have an effective system of quality checks. In other words, having a quality system does not always guarantee that a company will be a good supplier.

To be sure of your suppliers, you must make your own checks. That is why this is included in the standard. The standard does not force you to go and check; it merely says to evaluate and select suppliers based on your requirements. The action you take is at your discretion.

Again, that requirement is down to your intuition, professionalism and regard for your customers. Because if you do not check incoming supplies properly, depending on how critical those supplies are, how can you have a good regard for your customers?

If the products are nuts and bolts, then check a percentage based on importance at your premises, but at least check. If these parts are for an airline manufacturer or other significantly safety associated industries, then you may want to adjust your checking rate higher than an average percentage. Is that rate specified by *your* customers?

There are of course, other scoring factors. It could be the ability to meet production demands or price, quality of product or even the location of business. You may want to see their accounts and send your accountant. Maybe you think that they have too much custom and may sacrifice your product quality if they keep taking on orders that they cannot complete? These are just examples. What you have to do is evaluate them: the degree of evaluation is up to you.

I used to visit our suppliers when I worked elsewhere, I got on well with them and if you do this, you can usually get matters speeded up if you need something quicker than usual, suppliers will be open with you if you go and see them. You should be nice to them and treat them with respect. I got to know all of the quality managers and when we had an issue; it was easier for me to sort it out. On the other side I got to see other interesting businesses and meet really interesting people, plus it gets you out of your normal place of work and gives you a break from the norm.

Specified purchase requirements should be met. The auditor will look for this and for continuity from your orders.

Your suppliers really are important for your business activities, they are your life blood and you should control them at points of entry to your business. Some companies may send their own auditors and, from experience, these audits can be much worse that any auditor from a third party accrediting body. I have known a customer send some really troublesome auditors to ensure that a supplier is up to scratch. An auditor is there to test your system, not to cause trouble!

Unfortunately some auditors go over the top and can be too pedantic; the best auditors are the ones that cast an objective and impartial eye, and deliver their assessment with integrity and an approach that is co-operative.

The professional auditor knows when he has the required evidence of objective conformity or non-conformity; a positive auditor will always look to pass you and find evidence of conformity.

I shall explain more about auditing later on and what to look out for; it is a tender point with customers and auditors alike.

When an auditor is asking about your suppliers, it is best if you have some information and hard facts on them, rather than offering anecdotes and hearsay. Please remember that the standard is asking you for your criteria for selection and evaluation of suppliers; this should be recorded with records as indicated by the presence of 4.2.4 at the end of the paragraphs.

Purchasing information and verification of purchased product.

Purchasing information is important to the supplier and to you. It is extremely important that this information is consistent between the two parties and, where necessary, duplicated and used in separate parts of the receiving company.

What I mean by this is the stores may want and need a copy of purchase orders so that products coming into the company can be checked and ticked off when received.

When products are delivered, they can be checked against the delivery note and the person at the stores then knows that the products being received are genuine and possibly complete. If incomplete, then the store person may ask why. This can be queried before the delivery driver goes back to the supplier or elsewhere.

It's useful to have a stamp to mark the driver's delivery note. This stamp can say a number of things, 'accepted', 'goods checked', etc, but the message I prefer, especially when receiving lots of technical equipment or hundreds and thousands of parts, is the following. "Goods received but not checked for accuracy and integrity at present." This statement does two things: it says that you have received the goods, but also that you have not checked them as yet. It means that you have not formally accepted the parts as complete or accurate.

This is a good idea if you are receiving lots of products that cannot possibly be checked all at once. The consignment may require being broken down into smaller chunks to enable effective checking.

It is always a good idea to get the delivery driver to sign that the goods have been delivered, your staff to sign as having received (but not checked as yet), and the time and date. All this can clarify matters if an issue arises with the supplier.

The information about all purchasing aspects should be complete and it should be commensurate with what has been ordered. What I would do as an auditor would be to check the goods in paperwork and work backwards to the purchasing department to check to see what has been ordered.

You could do it the other way around of course, but you may not know if a certain delivery has been received. That is why I check goods in first, so I know that the received items can be checked properly against the purchasing information, I check to see if the two correspond.

Other purchasing information may include quality controlled instructions, which may be applied in the event of a supplier delivering unsatisfactory goods, which happens from time to time. This information is critical. If a check is to be made on materials and dimensions, then the quality control function at goods in (or just after) is vital; the sooner issues can be picked up, the more accurate can be the delivery times to *your* consumer.

Inspection is highly influential in determining how good your bought product is. The employees who carry out your inspections should be thorough, have an eye for detail and have a hands-on approach. They should be responsible individuals who can think for themselves and be able to take decisions commensurate with their posts to be able to determine if a product is satisfactory or not. Inspection is rightly regarded as a point of possible error, the part of the business which is the gateway to production. If any issues get missed here, sometimes production staff will assume that the goods have been checked properly so will be less likely to look out for faults when they are using the goods for processing.

Be sure to involve a manager at goods in points, to ensure that the quality of workmanship is upheld and monitored. If yours is a small company, get someone to check it as a part-time responsibility.

Another aspect of purchasing is qualification of personnel, which works in a number of ways. The first is that purchasing staff are properly trained or educated in their function, which is one of the most important parts of the business. More importantly, if a supplied product or service is being delivered by a member of staff (and this probably applies more to service), the person delivering the service must be appropriately trained or educated to deliver to the buyer.

If we take the case of an architect or surveyor working with a company as part of the design team (who is not directly employed by the purchasing company), they should be professionally educated in architecture or surveying and have the appropriate professional qualifications and experience.

There are many other purchasing directions with regards to qualification. The supplier of a service must ensure that their staff meet professional and trade-related requirements and qualifications before the service can be delivered effectively. Would you want a gas fitter mending your customer's gas cooker who was trained to install washing machines? Of course not, which is why the supplier of the goods or service must be appropriately qualified and / or experienced.

As a buyer of a product, you must ensure that your part of the bargain is clear: in giving your suppliers clear instruction when purchasing, or delivering if it is a service. As we have all seen time and again, the 'blame game' starts when the buyer is arguing with the supplier about a discrepancy for which neither is prepared to accept fault. You as the buyer have absolute responsibility that you provide the manufacturer or supplier with clear and concise instruction as to what you require from that product or service; anything other than that and you are failing yourselves. If the supplier then commits a fault, you have jurisdiction for claiming the rights.

When a product is to be delivered to a customer without verification at the supplier's own premises, the supplier must take all reasonable methods to check the goods at the customer's premises.

The arrangements must be clear and concise and you must have the approval (preferably recorded) as to the agreement that you have in place. This is usually apparent when dealing with a retailer. They purchase from a vendor, pass it straight onto the customer without opening the package or box, and have to provide written guarantees that the customer can exercise if the product is faulty. That is written confirmation of a verification arrangement. The arrangement is that the product is checked by the customer. You cannot possibly check all products if you are a retailer and you are passing on other companies' products, so you have to give them 28 days or similar for a possible return or refund. This period varies from country to country but is standard in the United Kingdom.

If you deliver straight to your customer, what can you do if the product bypasses your premises? One option is to send a quality manager or other member of your inspection team to the supplier and check a percentage of the goods before they are packed and sent, if this makes sense to do so, it depends on the product.

This way you check the goods before despatch, but you check them at your supplier's premises instead of your own. As long as you are being responsible, you are checking and you can prove this to the auditor. When I used to be a quality manager I used to go to companies and inspect their quality system and then the products, verifying a percentage of them. This worked well and you might be able to do the same.

Production and service provision

Control of production and service provision

Many people ask what this part of the standard means. Again, this is another aspect of the translation effect I spoke of earlier. I quite like the description. 'Control of production' is clear enough, while 'service provision' means 'arrangement or preparation beforehand, for the doing of something, the meeting of needs, the supplying of means, etc.

Now you understand that it is the delivery of your product it is concerned with, we can move on. This section is about what the company does to control its product or service and how it delivers it.

There are many aspects to this in different sectors and companies. However, the bottom line is how you control you product: is there any quality control that goes along with it? Do you provide instructions for the user(s)? Do you give them suitable equipment to do the job? Does it describe how the product behaves or has it any certain characteristics that the user may need to be aware of?

Do you need to monitor your production or service, and if so, how? Do you need staff to control the product or service? What are you going to ask them to do? How are you going to deliver the product to your customer and have you organised the delivery of it?

You may be thinking that this part is already carried out at your company; you will be right, but a lot of companies do not always monitor what they are doing or sort their deliveries out correctly. We have all complained about poor service in our lives.

Do you know the exact dates that the customer wants your product or service? Have you emailed or written to them and confirmed the arrangements, and did they agree? Have you spoken to them about it? If not, you should; the customer may want their goods or service a month earlier than you think. This all comes down to effective communication, which assists a great deal with this clause. A lot of this comes under planning.

This clause is very much about the heartbeat of your business, what you do, how you do it and how you control and instruct staff and machinery. Staff are there to be programmed, just like computers; and if you give them incorrect programming, your service provision will suffer.

I know that this sounds rather impersonal; programming is just for computers, right? No, our brains are programmed to receive information and to act upon it. A boss or work colleague may wish to programme our brains for work purposes. Training is a form of programming, as is any education or work instruction. People are programmed in a variety of ways; you just have to ensure that you are giving your staff the correct instructions and tools to do the job.

This programming should come in the form of work instruction of some kind. Work instructions are important in some forms of business; people unfamiliar with complex routines may require written procedures. Work instructions are also there as a point of contact or reference if a person needs to refer to a document because they are unsure. These instructions must be available at points of use, not stuck in your quality manual or computer.

That is a very important part of service provision: work instructions should always be available to whoever needs them. They should be easily found by the person who needs them most, usually the workforce. The auditor may check and ask if relevant instructions are given to the users and staff and if they are controlled. To give an example, if there was a work instruction for the goods inwards area and I went there, I would expect to see it.

Work instructions do not always have to be controlled though; it depends on what it relates to. If the instruction is always changing because of constant process updates etc, a controlled format should be available and revised to show any updated inputs. If the updating of a revision is not controlled, this can cause serious problems to your workings and product. People may be carrying out instructions that have changed. This is not their fault, it is the reviser's responsibility. Many companies update their quality systems but do not bother informing the people affected.

If a work instruction is uncontrolled, it may be because there is only one valid way of carrying out a process. Therefore the document may be there as a referring book if you are unsure of the process, it may help to train new staff and provide familiarisation points.

Whatever the form of instruction, I believe that it is far better to keep them controlled by engineers or staff, because it helps in controlling production or service. It assists in retaining the control of your work.

Equipment must be suitable for the task. If your Directors are overly reluctant to spend money in this area, it can cause problems. Let me be clear: I am a big fan of fiscal prudence and keeping a tight rein of financial expenditure. A lot of companies spend far too much on the wrong types of asset or third party services, and are walking a tightrope as a result. However where there is a need to provide the correct equipment, it really should be in place. If you cannot afford the best quality then you have to make do with what is in your financial range.

There is a compensation factor here, which is well trained staff. Excellent staff often get companies out of the mire through their technical excellence when faced with inferior production equipment. That will resonate with many an engineer or production worker.

Organisations have to 'make do' sometimes, and occasionally we have to make the best of the tools that we have got. At other times, we really need a piece of kit to do the best job. It's down to your organisation. If you do buy new equipment however, use a suitably qualified person to trial it and to teach others. It's always best to use your personnel's strengths.

If you have new equipment, the auditor may ask you how you tested it and who carried the testing out. These are reasonable questions, and you should be able to answer easily if you have carried out the correct procedures in commissioning new equipment.

This clause is about your staff, your equipment, your monitoring and your delivery activities. Look at your systems and see if they need strengthening. If they do, always carry this out with the input and approval of others.

Validation of processes for production and service provision

This clause is very particular, because it is asking the organisation if it has employed any 'special processes' in order to validate its work before receipt. Because the product can only be truly tested upon full use.

So what do we mean by 'special processes' or 'validation'? A validation is a way of ensuring that the product is satisfactorily tested before delivery by choosing a variety of methods to test it, before it is accepted by the customer. If you check the wording of the standard, it says that deficiencies may only become apparent after delivery, which can affect any product of course.

With this in mind, the company can employ 'special' processes to check the work while it is in production. If the company carries out any extra testing or service provision that goes above the normal quality controlled application, that would come under this clause.

What might be deemed a special process or validation? Let me take an example of an engineering company producing steel beams and an assembly for a petrochemical business, where the filtration of petroleum and gas is used within a tower or large vessel.

To get the right quality of a material, the engineering company must check that the correct analysis is taking place in order to verify the accuracy of the supplied product that they are using. They may use what is known as non-destructive testing. This testing takes place and analyses the material before use. The beams (Rolled Steel Joists or RSJs) are bolted together and built at the customer's premises, and it is only then that the beams are subjected to force, other chemicals and materials that 'may' affect the build quality. The structure cannot be proven until the product has been installed at the customer's premises and put under huge stresses and strains.

The organisation has to ensure that it checks the beams and structure as rigorously as possible in order to get the quality 100 per cent correct before installing the assembly into its vessel. This way, the customer should be satisfied that all reasonable measures have been concluded before accepting the item.

The supplier could apply forces and chemicals away from the premises using identical test pieces and using arenas that are not far from the conditions that it may encounter when delivery has taken place, it may also come as a result of experience in the field. The example is to highlight the issue and to ask yourselves if anything 'special' is required at your organisation, or what do you already employ that fulfils this part of the standard?

The processing of products in your premises must be accurate. If a deficiency is uncovered after delivery, you must ensure that all corrective processes are accurate and re-proven or revalidated.

The equipment that you may use will be a massively important factor. It should be calibrated and accurate. You may need to test that piece of equipment every time you use it, or it may self-calibrate. Staff who use this equipment will be well trained, be able to self-diagnose and be adept at identifying and analysing results. They should be competent in their fields and have the necessary qualifications and experience to back this up.

When special processes or validatory processes are required, it is highly important that your organisation displays an integral process that matches the importance of that product, because the product will only really be tested upon receipt by the customer, so it may be up to you to test thoroughly before receipt?

Your validatory activities should be well planned, correctly executed, use well trained and educated staff, and be well tested. Revalidation must occur and it must be coherent with applied standards that you must set.

If you have to test equipment that you are manufacturing or using, ask yourself what is it that needs to be tested. Where are the weak pieces within the components? What is most vulnerable to force, chemicals, exploitation or sabotage? The latter is one area that companies are becoming more familiar with, sadly. It happens; and this clause is all about protecting your product. Remember, if your quality procedures break down, your company will suffer as a result. This clause is highly important if it applies to your organisation.

All of the clauses in this standard are applied for good reason, and their importance and usefulness are well proven.

If you need to validate, revalidate or prove your product before delivery. The motto here is test, test and test again before you pass the product on. If you test material and products under applied and similar circumstances, make sure that your customer sees the depth that you are going to. You could even ask for their approval on this – I certainly would.

Identification and traceability

How do you identify your products, your supplies and your customers? How do you label your products? Is that down to component level? Is it with references, is it numbers, letters, or a combination?

What about testing and analysis: if you carry this out, do the referencing aspects match up to the job? Do you identify which equipment was used in manufacture or production? If you have 100 machines, all of them the same make and model, do you have local serial numbers that could be used to identify a machine if something went wrong? Is this information replicated on production sheets, etc?

What about paperwork and references to jobs and contracts: does it all match up? Are customer references all in place? Does your customer want you to have a referencing system that they themselves use and know? Some customers will want you to use their identification marks.

The questions above are designed to make you think about the reference aspects in your organisation. Referencing is truly important if you do not want to end up in a confused world of work.

Identification and traceability is a clause that is scrutinised well on audits throughout the audit without actually being mentioned very much. This is because the auditor will be following the well known 'audit trail' or 'paperwork trail' – as some like to call it. By following the trails by paperwork and organisational documents, auditors can find their way about your system and audit it properly.

If an auditor is constantly asking you where things are, and you are scrabbling around trying to piece together information, it is highly likely that you will contravene this part of the standard.

When an auditor visits your premises and looks at your quality manual, he may see references that you have inserted into the text that relate to other parts of your management system and business. The auditor may see numbers and references to different variants of paperwork relevant to your organisation. When the auditor goes to check which paperwork that you have referenced, is it traceable? Can you provide the evidence?

In purchasing, for instance, do you just buy products without correctly referencing to the contract that you are buying them for? If there is no contract to buy them for, do you have purchase order numbers to log the information?

In an organisation, there are so many ways to prove this part of the standard – and so many ways to fall foul of it. Personnel files can sometimes get mixed up, for instance. If you have people's records they should be held separately, in a folder or envelope with their name on it.

When we put this clause into a manufacturing context it starts to get more complicated. This is because when manufacturing and assembling equipment, traceability of parts when putting together an assembly is vital, especially if there are numerous parts and they carry out numerous functions.

I have come across organisations that laser etch design references onto their parts; when the parts are fitted together the component is identifiable. This helps the technician assembling the parts, it gives the designer something to identify with and it gives the customer important information regarding their purchase.

Drawing references are important: sometimes on a detailed drawing you cannot possibly have every part named or identified, so what tends to happen is that the parts are given a number. This number should then correspond to the same number in the title block somewhere at the foot of the drawing, or maybe on an information drawing or information sheet related to that product and drawing. This is so that the designer, assembly staff, user and customer can see how the product is fitted together. Occasionally the customer may not want to know this information, but you should still include an assembly drawing of some kind.

Let's take this application one stage further. Should companies such as those manufacturing or selling furniture for houses reference those parts and give you a detailed design so that you can assemble the product? Yes, of course. But we've all been there, complaining about the vast number of screws and accessories that with the product – not to mention the confusing diagram and instructions!

Traceability and identification are so important in our everyday lives. We need to recognise the products we are selling or buying. If every time you went to the supermarket you found your favourite products labelled differently, you would not be happy.

Your organisation should do what it thinks that it should in delivering the requirements of this clause relating to the questions that you should ask yourselves at the start of this section. You must ensure that everything has a marker or indication if it relates to important information and detail. You must decide what is important and what needs identifying and tracing. You can bet if there is a weakness in this area, the auditor will find it.

Customer property

If you use customer property for any reason, you should treat it with respect and care just as if it were your own. Customer's property is usually loaned or leased to you for a variety of reasons and can include many assets.

Customer property can be in many forms and can include drawings, technical data and specifications, copyrighted material, instructions, information technology hardware and software, data, personal data and company information, tools, equipment, accessories, special jigs (to fit an assembly securely in a bespoke fashion), paperwork, management systems, vehicles, machinery, testing equipment, licences, welfare and recreational facilities, buildings, accommodation, support frameworks and anything else that you have a duty of care over from your customer.

The above could also include people, staff, temporary workers that may be loaned out to your company to assist you. I know that it sounds a bit impersonal, but if you look at it in another sense, such people are under your duty of care (while being paid for by your customer, yourselves or a third party). You have a duty of care to them as well, especially for their health and safety and welfare.

In a personnel instance, you should provide them with protective equipment, risk assessments and method statements, work instructions and appropriate health care and monitoring if required.

This duty of care applies, irrespective of standards. For the purpose of this clause, we will be looking at the asset list.

Customer property if under your care must be correctly looked after. This may include servicing, testing, calibration and maintenance. It could involve licences and agreements, especially in the case of software use. Software licences from customers may come under scrutiny if effective care is not placed upon them. Such licences are easily abused with the material getting into the wrong hands. It would be difficult to prove on audit regarding copying but software should be kept under lock and key. If an auditor sought your software and you declared that it was the ownership of your customer, they will probably want know where it is kept and the details of the licence.

When implementing ISO 9001, a lot can be overlooked. Remember, when that auditor comes to visit your premises, s/he can ask many reasonable business questions. This could involve anything that involves your business which is applicable to the standard in order to pass.

When you allow auditors into your premises, you are effectively opening your business up – with the notable exception of finances and accounts, unless you give the auditor jurisdiction on this matter and you have purposely included it into the framework of your quality management system.

The property that you are using should be identifiable and records will be available if you lose or damage the property or if it is unsuitable for reasons that may be disclosed. The reason that the standard asks for a record is if there is any damage or issue, because there may be legal and statutory repercussions.

It obviously depends on the issue, but as the representative of a responsible organisation, you should be taking every reasonable step to ensuring that this does not happen again. You should also satisfy your customer that you have either fixed the equipment, have a replacement, returned it under agreement or give them appropriate recompense for any damaged goods.

This does not apply to all cases of customer property, however. In the case of personal customer company data for instance, the company may have an even bigger problem if that information is compromised.

Personal data use (and more importantly misuse) is an increasingly hot topic. I personally consult on the information security standard, ISO | IEC 27001. It is amazing what details some companies hold about you. If you are a retailer and your shoppers buy from you online, as an auditor I would want to see the Data Protection Act being enforced properly. There are a myriad opportunities in this part of the standard to control.

If you lose customer information and that same information falls into the hands of unscrupulous activities, you could be prosecuted and fined. So when you think that your computer records of your customers are unimportant, think again. Are your computers encrypted? This is useful, because if the equipment was stolen the chances of a hard disk becoming unencrypted and the information compromised are minimal. Do your accounts computers and other customer (information holding) computers have passwords to access them? Is there full disk encryption in place? Are the files partially encrypted? With Microsoft's new bit locker encryption system, computers have built-in technology to further safeguard your assets. If you're not using this, you might want to start.

Now that we have explored this section thoroughly, you may think that customer property is a bit more than a piece of equipment or a test piece. And you would be right.

In this technologically advanced era, customer property also includes electronic information. Please do not overlook this; customer details are often easy to steal or tamper with, so take measures to prevent these things happening.

Preservation of product

The product that you are manufacturing, delivering or assembling must be preserved for the customer. 'Preserved' means delivered to your customer in a manner that is satisfactory to the customer. Your product must be fully protected in process, storage, transit, delivery, when it is being prepared for and being used.

That last stage is the one that organisations tend to overlook; preservation is not just about storage and delivery. The standard talks about identification, handling, packaging, storage and protection. When the product is finally delivered to your customer, the protection element comes under scrutiny.

A quality product may last for years, obviously depending on the usage factor, sector, type of use and so forth. If we take motor car manufacture as an example, Audi and BMW certainly build their cars to last. They use advanced paint protection in the paintwork, they afford the engine a high degree of capability and engineering build factor. They give out warranties that protect the lifespan of their product and they ensure that their product is adequately protected. It's then up to the customer to take care of it.

Obviously other costs come into this; but when those cars come off the production line, they are usually in pristine condition. Other manufacturers carry out similar activities; I use Audi and BMW because I believe that they stand out in their engineering discipline and product quality.

Perhaps many footballers would do well to follow some of the preservation techniques used by the German footballers! German international footballers look after themselves with the highest of disciplines, they preserve their bodies *and* brains, hone their muscles to delivering for their customer – the German nation.

German beer is subject to a purity law, so that it is naturally preserved and not contaminated or tainted with chemicals. German beer is recognised as being amongst the best in the world. Why? Because it is well preserved. The same applies to Scotch Whisky, a quality product that relies on a precious foundation of preservation that has served for centuries, often in the hands of caring family firms. Guinness brewed in Ireland is another example. Many punters suggest that Irish Guinness is far better than the same product brewed elsewhere. And that's maybe because of traditional preserved methods that serve well through time. I'd have to agree!

You might ask how this clause can be applied to your organisation. In other words, what is the Audi or BMW preservation factor in your business product? The customer does not want to hear excuses. If you manufactured motor cars, would you carefully deliver each car and protect it from damage? Or would you just take it by tow truck to its destination and not bother to clean it up on delivery to your important customer?

For British engineering, I look to the glorious past of Brunel, Stephenson and Telford. These and others like them built bridges and steam engines to stand the test of time, steam engines and trains that are as good or maybe better than modern ones constructed today. But what has happened? Preservation has possibly been sacrificed at the altar of mismanagement and cost cutting? Virgin Trains are however, a great leader in resurrecting that past on our railways and have a modern approach and heartfelt vision with the fabulous Pendolino trains.

Some of our home grown UK products are outstripped by others, for the sake of cost cutting and profits. There is a market for everybody, though. What does your organisation do to ensure that your product or service is suitably protected?

You have to look at your organisation and decide what needs to be afforded the relevant protection to preserve its status as a quality product. Is it individual parts or the assembly as a whole? Do you speak to your suppliers if they deliver your supplies in a manner not consistent with your good all round business practice?

Supplies are one of the areas that come under scrutiny on audit. I have seen the most precious of steel parts thrown together in a box and delivered to a business without any thought to their integrity and completeness from the vendor or sender. That is just plain wrong: here is where quality really is a product issue rather than a quality assurance issue.

If you let your suppliers deliver your products in an unacceptable manner, if you let them get away with not protecting your items, you are failing your customers. Your customers will take out their issues with you, not on your suppliers.

This brings us onto another part of the preservation discussion. If you deliver your product in a sub-standard fashion, if you don't protect it in some way you could be heading for trouble? As an example you may require bubble wrap, protective coverings, cloths, cushioning, oxygen-reduced atmospheres for it to sit in, or a moisture controlled packaging with desiccant present to reduce humidity, the characteristics of your product could change. That in turn could change your customer's perception of you, it is up to you to decide what method suits your product, you may already be doing it?

Ignore product protection throughout processing and delivery and you are ignoring your customers. If you do so, quality quickly becomes rubbish.

What good is your product without suitable protection? Whether that be from your suppliers to you, throughout the process, storage, delivery and throughout customer use, it is vital to get that right. Organisations, companies, businesses and practices are all judged on this factor.

You frequently hear about bad products: those which don't last, are of poor quality or break down quickly. There is no need to name names; no doubt you could think of some examples right now. The question is, do you want your organisation to be in this bracket? Obviously not.

This part of the standard does more for you than nearly any other. It is also a part that will make you look foolish should you choose to ignore it if your product requires a high degree of protection. If it comes down to cost, what can you do with what you can afford? Afford your products the best protection you can.

Perhaps if preservation of product should be renamed "Preservation and care of organisational product and reduction of misuse", maybe more people would sit up and listen when it comes to this massively important section.

The thing that you now have to decide upon is how to apply it into the framework of your business. You may already do so; but in most cases you can maybe do more. There will always be something that is out of place, nothing is perfect. You may have to ensure that you reduce those risks to your product further? Or, it could just be perfect as it is?

Control of monitoring and measuring equipment

Depending on your organisation, monitoring and measuring equipment can include many different aspects that are viable and important.

When we take this clause into consideration it can cover, to start with the most obvious, any monitoring or measuring equipment that you have in order to ensure that your product or service is kept intact, accurate and helps you to conform to requirements.

In your organisation, what do you have that measures? More importantly, what do you need to measure? Do you use the appropriate controls to do so? If you don't, you and an expert in the field must get your heads together and form a plan of action.

This monitoring and measuring equipment can come in many guises: Vernier calipers, Vernier protractors, micrometers, depth gauges, CNC (Computer Numerically Controlled) machinery, feeler gauges, laser measuring devices, Brinell or Vickers hardness testers, temperature monitors, humidity controls, CO_2 and carbon monoxide monitoring, other gas analysers, noise and decibel ratings, spectrum analysers, multi-meters and oscilloscopes, chemical analysers and material disposition probes, non destructive testing and analysis machines, computer hardware and software...the list is enormous. It could include almost anything, especially software that has been designed for your product to ensure that its quality is meeting exacting standards and requirements.

In the instance of tape measures and rules, of any type and length, they should be controlled with an element of common sense. I believe that you can control them by giving to your staff rules and tape measures that are approved and examined. I also recommend that they be checked to see that their ends are intact, the numbers readable and of a consistent nature. There is not a great deal that you can do apart from that. I would give them a local serial and note who owns it, and check them every six or 12 months. If an auditor asks you how do you calibrate them, tell him to stop being silly. Calibration is where you can change an input to achieve a desired output, can you alter a tape or rule? No. If it's ruined, buy a new one.

I suggest you stress that staff should not bring in their own measuring equipment, even if it a favourite rule or piece of equipment that they "have always used". On many audits, I see people using much more of their own equipment than just rules; you need to put a stop to this for the sake of your quality control. Provide decent equipment, and people will be happy to use company products instead of their own. Ask them what makes their personal equipment more attractive and efficient to use and see if you can get your organisation to purchase them too. This will go down well with your peers as you are trying to help them.

If we look at more manual measures like engineering squares and slip gauges to check pieces of equipment, we can save ourselves a bit of money and time by checking them ourselves. I used to keep an 8 inch engineer's square to check all the other 4, 5 & 6 inch squares that we used. It came with a certificate and I kept it safely in my drawer. It was highly accurate. I would test other squares against this and if gaps appeared, I would specify the accuracy with feeler gauges; 1mm out at the very inside corner of a square may translate into a possible 10 millimetre error at 1 metre. If your square is out, to what accuracy are you working? You should specify those limits with a work instruction that details how measurements are taken and made and what the tolerance is.

The same applies to slip gauges. They will be manufactured to a high standard and should come with their own test certificates including tolerances and temperatures at which they are accurately measured. If you check your micrometers and Vernier calipers at such a level of accuracy with these gauges, a simple slip gauge set can save you the trouble and money of using a test house.

Sometimes testing needs to take place in 19 / 20 °C (68 °F) conditions, because of the coefficient of thermal expansion of the metal. This can be influential at certain temperatures, depending on what you are measuring and what is measuring it. You may need a controlled room or laboratory conditions to carry out your calibrations - depending on the criticality of your product?

It is the same with any measuring and monitoring equipment: you should be highlighting those limits that are specified in respect of what you need to be measuring, measuring against them, have records that show your accuracy and also have records when something fails and is scrapped.

In an engineering environment, scrapping of items will be common in a workshop, so if you say that you haven't scrapped an item in ten years, the auditor may become suspicious. In quality circles it is right to highlight problems and get over them by debate and corrective action rather than covering up something that may happen again.

Calibrating of equipment should be in evidence. If you use a testing house, what is their certification and evidence for being able to perform functionality analysis? The test house should prove its credentials and you should show the auditor who you use and what the results of any testing are.

Calibration techniques may show adjustments and further controls that have been applied to ensure accuracy.

Finally, for all equipment, testing should be done regularly to see that it still functions correctly.

Computer software may need to be tested too depending on its application and nature as they are used a lot for processes nowadays. Its diagnosis should be performed at specific intervals. It could be carried out by recognised professionals whose competence can be proved to the auditors. This software will match to the requirements of the manufacturer and should follow specific instructions. If it is bespoke software then you may need to identify what methods are used for calibration and the people who performed it.

This section is easily adapted to your organisation. First, take account of the controlling of your assets company side and making a note of what they do, where they do it and how important it is to your organisation. You can decide amongst your staff what the requirements are for calibration and testing. An asset register may also help here.

We have now covered, three quarters of the standard, section 7 is a massive part of it, so you are well on your way to completing your implementation!

13.   Managing and analysing your processes

Measurement, analysis and improvement is 8.0 in the standard.

General

This section is all about the aspects of a management system that can be looked at when it is all running and everything is starting to fit into place.

On implementation, this section will naturally evolve throughout the proactive nature of practising what you are preaching in your procedures and instructions in some instances. You are starting to check your processes and procedures and that they are working correctly, and make any changes where they are not.

For a start, you analyse and measure by reviewing your system, which is then backed up by analysing at management review, internal audit etc. As I mentioned before, some parts of the standard are easily covered by other parts too: clause 5.6 Management Review and 8.2.2 internal audit are prime examples of this. When you satisfy some parts of the standard, you may also satisfy other parts if you do them correctly.

What of your processes do you need to analyse and measure? This is where someone's experience may be key and speaking to different departments and sections will help you.

What is important in this clause is that you look at your QMS and decide what is going right or wrong. If you analyse your quality objectives on the quality policy, you should be able to analyse each year if you have achieved your goals and / or the organisation is reaching its goals too. If you use the quality policy correctly, review it once per year and change your goals to suit. That is analysing. Keeping a nice fresh quality policy also goes a long way to achieving other parts of the standard.

Continual improvement of the standard can easily be achieved by implementing the matters highlighted on audit. It can also be the same with management review. Finding out what is not quite right and putting it correct is a part of measurement, analysis and improvement.

The main part of this section is the highlighting of your processes and monitoring what is going on in your organisation. You have to decide how best to do this. The easiest way is to ask those involved if everything that you are carrying out and introducing is working. Are people happy with any alterations to the business model made for the sake of a quality management system?

It is worth noting that not all systems and procedures should be changed or altered to suit; sometimes the finest quality management systems are based on already proven systems of work. Sometimes, it is unnecessary to change any parts of a business. In my experience, though, there is always something to add, some benefit that can be gained, which is our goal here.

The best implementation in my view comes through using methods already employed by the organisation and adding to them where required. Don't add a new system just for the sake of it. The saying "if it isn't broke, don't fix it," is as true of management systems as it is of machinery.

The process of analysis and measurement can be carried out with a variety of methods, some of which will already exist in your organisation. These will be tests of some kind, graphical data, data tables, discussions between staff. Emails, meetings and minutes of those meetings, design matters – these are all part of analysis. It is highly likely that you already doing most of these things. As long as you measure your processes, get data to prove that the processes are working (or not), have internal audits and management reviews, have safety meetings and other meetings, the chances are that this part will just fall into place. My advice is to get some graphical data of your processes (if you can) or data into tables too, to show the auditor that it's not just audits and reviews you use analysis on, have something concrete for them to look at.

For some organisations however, more can be required. Testing and analysis of ship manufacture, aircraft, motor vehicles, trains and anything else that needs stringent analysis, could have a massive bearing on the result on audit. There must be a recognised form of testing and analysis in place if this is the case. Maybe there is a standard to help you with this in your organisation; it's worth finding out.

So whatever your business, think to yourself, what is it that we need to measure and check to see that our processes are correct? What can we do to gain a competitive edge? How can our business be progressed by measuring and analysing elements of it?

Monitoring and measurement: Customer satisfaction

This section should be pretty easy for most of us; after all, speaking to customers and receiving a satisfied response is pretty common, isn't it?

Actually, it isn't as common as you might expect. Most of the companies I speak to do not always engage with their customers much and ask them if everything is satisfactory after delivery. The reason for this lack of communication is varied and sometimes hard to fathom. What is not in doubt, though, are that your customers are vital to your business – and satisfying them is essential if that business is to survive, let alone grow.

One of the best sales tactics is to ask your current customers what you can do better. There are many ways to do this, but most companies now seem to opt for questionnaires. We have all seen them; they're usually far too long, and we're usually too busy to complete them.

So let's leave such nineteenth century technology aside. The best way today is to use online methods. You could send a word document or PDF to your customers and ask them if they can spare a minute to answer a few questions, scan it and send it back to you. However, even that can be a chore for some.

Microsoft seems to have got this area pretty wrapped up. It uses online surveys that don't take long to fill out. Some companies try to induce you by offers of gifts to get that valued information.

This feedback is important and forward thinking companies know this. Many people are more honest in an online survey and those that do take the time to do it are far likelier to provide value.

However, we can't all design online surveys so we should settle for the next best thing: email five to seven questions to your customer representative and tell them you will telephone on this day at this time for an answer. This method, in my experience, usually works best.

This approach does two things. It tells the person their input is highly valued, and it tells them that you are serious about your quest for improvement.

If you tell your customer that this will take five minutes of their time, you agree when to call and that will be it for them, you will take the notes and they just have to answer! However, this doesn't guarantee honesty; some clients will just tell you what you want to hear. Others, though, will be eager to tell you what they think and be keen to help you with constructive comment.

So now you have the feedback. What about scoring? I would ask some direct questions that they can give an answer in numbers: for example, how would you rate our service, from one (terrible) to five (outstanding)? You can then ask them to provide details from their experiences, which will naturally force them to think and evaluate the question before answering. This can be a great solution and give detailed responses.

For example, if you are a retailer and you have products sent back that may be faulty, the wrong size or even broken, this may result in a credit note or refund of some kind or even a replacement product. Whatever it is you should log it, to help you spot trends. Have they made a customer complaint? Have you a process for complaints and how are they dealt with?

Customer complaints procedures are very beneficial to have. In any organisation that I consult with I always ensure that they have this in place to cover the standard. Have you a procedure for dealing with those complaints? You'll need one, a quick A4 form and accompanying instructions on the reverse can be enough.

When a customer complains, as some invariably do, you have a system with dealing with it and all corrective actions can be detailed properly, instead of leaving someone to write it on a piece of paper that they will lose, or an email that they cannot find.

I would certainly have a complaints system; and I would also have a scoring system for feedback coupled with a quick questionnaire.

This clause is relatively straightforward, in my experience, people are reluctant to do this initially. I guess that once people have made a sale they move on to the next target. I think we are all guilty of this, so take a moment, devise a satisfaction procedure that is right for you and you should be fine. You do not have to contact every customer, be choosy if you like? Just explain to the auditor your reasons for doing so. Is it one in five, one in ten, or maybe more you'd like to contact? You could have hundreds of thousands of clients each year, depending on your product and service, deal with a percentage to get your results.

Internal audit

This part of the standard requires a documented procedure, which is mandatory. Internal auditing will be discussed in section 14.

Monitoring and measurement of processes

Monitoring and measurement of product

This clause is specific: monitoring and measuring of your processes and products can only be completed with a knowledge of how you should approach the measurement of a process, a product or a subject.

What processes do you have in your business that could be monitored? What do they involve and is there any way in which they could benefit from being monitored?

Common sense is a useful attribute to apply to this standard; especially, knowing the timing of a certain input of measurement can help you. What you shouldn't do is start to measure something that may not be welcomed, such as people's time management: that should be left for senior management to implement as part of a time and motion study. The clause explicitly mentions processes.

The standard talks of the need for 'planned results'. I know that sounds a little shallow, but really it keeps things nice and simple. If you are designing a product and the end result is a perfectly designed and manufactured item, is that not a planned result? Yes it is. What about your training programme: does that give you planned results when an employee uses their knowledge acquired on the courses to help the business improve? Yes it does.

The standard refers to the need to monitor quality management processes: you can do this at internal audits or management reviews. The measurement or monitoring of a process is not just about a time or calculation or measurement. It can be about simple notes, taking stock of what a process is achieving and seeing how a product can be improved.

Where a process is being measured, have you any corrective actions to present and to help you to improve your processes? Especially if you have encountered difficulties as a result of monitoring?

The clause must be applied to your organisation. Only you can determine what is needed to be measured.

The approach when discussing measurement of a product is slightly different. Measuring and monitoring of your product could be very detailed, possibly requiring assistance from a national or international standard for guidance. Excellent systems of guidance and codes of practice can be highly influential when trying to improve the characteristics and durability of your products.

What can be achieved by monitoring in your business product? Maybe it would be best to discuss this in some depth with your staff. If you are monitoring a process or a product already, is that not something to use? You do not have to monitor all processes but it would be beneficial in implementing a system of measurement in a critical component of your business.

You may discover different stress levels of a product. It could have characteristics and properties that you may not have even considered, but which come to light as a result of monitoring.

Remember that your customer may wish to see monitoring and measurement results. Have you asked them which monitoring process they require? If you do not ask them, there may be something hidden away in a contract that you do not know about. I would say to my customers, what would you like to see measured? There is nothing wrong in this, and most customers would be pleased that you are taking care with their product.

This monitoring could use any of the following subjects:

- Properties under pressure

- Properties under stress and strain

- Properties under temperature

- Properties under humidity

- Properties under time applications

- Properties as a result of varying chemicals being applied

- Properties as a result of different experiments that could add or remove certain factors.

The monitoring should be carried out at stages that are important in the realisation of your product. Are there any stages at your organisation that require highlighting because a greater emphasis has been placed upon them?

Maybe the use of a quality plan for a product or process would be beneficial to you? A quality plan can help you to pull people together, and act as a reminder that certain monitoring processes must be carried out.

Your organisation may also wish to develop its own quality plans and initiatives to supplement its procedures, works instructions and monitoring processes. It may help to control certain activities (especially in engineering and manufacturing) and will give a further level of quality assurance and control over the output of your organisation.

Quality plans usually detail a process that has been set out as a way of consolidating past successes by using applied monitoring that has been proven. What has worked in previous contracts may be worth pursuing in the next one. A system of quality built up over time will add value to the business and help to reduce customer problems and complaints. It will also give an overseeing eye a reference guide to follow and ensure that certain matters have been carried out and completed.

ISO 10005 - Guidelines for quality plans was issued to provide guidance on this subject and is extremely useful for particular work projects.

Because of the nature of business, every procedure may be different from organisation to organisation; a quality plan that has been well researched and used may be worthwhile in your organisation for your monitoring and measurement.

In the case of software, the plan may be used to facilitate management of a product. Certain checkpoints may have to be completed throughout its manufacture.

What should be considered when designing your quality plans?

- What the plan is used for.
- What value it can bring.
- Responsibilities of staff.
- National or international standards to be applied.
- The preferred sequence of events.
- Check points or quality points.
- Authorities and signatories.
- Consulting with the customer.
- Documents to be used for recording.
- Issues and revisions of documents to be used.

Without doubt, this will help you; you need to decide which is the best route to take for your organisation.

Control of nonconforming product

This part of the standard requires a documented procedure, which is mandatory.

Control of non-conforming product can be done easily if you set yourself up with the correct framework and reporting system.

Firstly, a non-conforming product could be the result of a few inputs. It could be from your supplies, perhaps delivered incorrectly in some way. It could be from internal processes: does something happen during processing? Has someone damaged a product? Or is it a customer problem? Has your customer supplied you with incorrect information; is there a discrepancy of detail between two parties? It could be a sub-contractor issue if you sub-contract work. There are many inputs; it all comes down to your format of business and what processes are in place.

Non-conforming product is not just the responsibility of the quality manager, but of every person in your organisation. The best advice I can give involves five pieces of a jigsaw that you may need to consider.

The first is a system of reporting, whether a paperwork system, computerised system or a mixture. What is important is to get the details logged by anybody who comes into contact with the product. Keep it simple and effective to your business. Maybe you don't need streams of paper; I encourage people to start by using one side of A4 paper with details on the other side.

The second is where are you going to put the product or segregate it? Are there any constraints to segregation? Are there dangers or health and safety measures to be considered, is there a place of safety to use for this occasion, and who needs to know?

What about contact numbers for emergency services and local non-emergency contacts that you may need if something goes wrong? Do you tell people who they should contact? Is there a list?

The ISO 14001 and BS OHSAS 18001 standards covers emergency preparedness and response much better than the ISO 9001 standard, in section 4.4.7 emergency preparedness and response. Maybe take a look at one of the standards and see if there is anything that you may require that can add value to your business too.

However, in my opinion, maybe you could use this clause from those standards too. Who needs to know if there is a problem? Where is the emergency kit? What are the contact details for line management or senior management? Does the local authority or environmental agency need to know? What about the Water board, Health and Safety Executive, etc? These are all good points for you to consider. It all depends on the non-conformance.

How are you going to go about this non-conformity process if you have no system? The quick way is training and discussion. Get people together from different departments and discuss this, then form a system that you all agree with and you can take the matter from there. It really can be that simple.

I suggest that you take basic details first, which could include:

- Product / service.

- Description.

- Date findings made.

- Batch number (if applicable).

- Supplier / Internal / Customer - whose fault could it possibly be?

- Whose counsel do you need to seek for rectification?

- Person reporting the matter.

- Nature of the problem?

- Are there problems with other products?

- Is there an instruction of where to send the report form to?

- Who needs to know?

- Are there procedures attached to certain non-conformities?

- Customer concessions.

This list is designed to help you think about how you can make it fit into your organisation. You can choose a mixture if you do not need everything mentioned, it covers most of what you may need.

The third step is who needs to be involved? The more people know about a problem, the quicker it can be fixed. Yes, I understand that sometimes it may be better not to tell somebody for private reasons: but companies need formal methods in place and a procedure to cover this scenario.

Does a director need to be involved? Is there a contact number? Is there guidance on what to fill in or a template that has been filled in to show staff how to do it? All of these are worth considering.

The fourth matter is what are you doing about it? Is there a certain level of non-conformance and guidance as to what goes wrong if somebody is on nights? This is a good point: when there are shifts in place, is there a system for reporting? Who is to be contacted in the event of a serious product or service issue?

Who needs to fix this issue, does the customer need to know? Depending on the seriousness of the non-conforming product, if a customer needs to know, isn't this best to leave this to a director? Get senior management's approval before shouting your problems to customers.

Finally, what needs to be considered to stop this happening again? Is this a quick fix or a permanent solution? If the former, I suggest a reporting format to keep on top of what needs to be done. The format should involve something like this:

- What is the problem and how is it logged? See previous list.

- Where is the product segregated?

- Who needs to know?

- What needs to be done to fix this non-conformance?

- What needs to be done to stop recurrence?

If the customer is to give concessions, who is to seek this concession? Under what boundaries does this concession exist and do you get written customer approval in some form? That last part is crucial. Customer acceptance on a non-conforming product will be paramount; they need to acknowledge that such a product is not part of the agreed terms and conditions.

As usual, records shall be present: in the case of a product requiring re-verification from the customer, this record will be especially important.

In the case of a service, if a member of staff performs in an uncontrolled manner leading to a non-conforming process, what are the procedures in place to deal with this? Are extra personnel required? What is the reporting system? Many ideas can only be found in your organisation.

What I have provided will help to give you some idea of what the auditor is searching for, what will help your business to succeed and to help you in business further.

Analysis of data

Your organisation shall collect information and data that will assist your organisation in maintaining its quality management system and the effectiveness of your operations.

There are many ways that an organisation can complete this task. It is down to the individual processes and how you view them. You must of course ensure that the system that now represents your organisational management system is suitable and effective. What you can ensure is that you analyse data in a way that brings a contribution and, where necessary, the appropriate changes.

Analysis is carried out by internal auditing and management review; however, you have to include data on this subject.

I advise people to have an action plan of improvements. This helps them to focus on what needs to be done and it is straight to the point. It is also highly useful because it removes any complex details. It highlights the problems that require addressing and gives a focal point. I analyse this with my clients at management review. When we have analysed the information I can then generate a five to seven page management review that has plenty of substance to it. (Auditors are sometimes unimpressed by management reviews that run to only one or two pages in one year).

Analysis of the audits should also be clear on the review. What non-conformities are there? What did the external audit raise? What are we doing about it and who is responsible?

It does not stop there: customer satisfaction records have to be viewed. What are the comments or scores, what is to be done about it and who needs to be involved? All of this analysis should take place at management review and it should be thorough and detailed.

Product conformity is another area that you must generate your results from. Analysis should be carried out throughout your processing. What should you be analysing? Your product and process outputs are the most obvious; you must decide what those outputs are and what is the most relevant. What needs checking? It could be analysis of welding calibration, properties or your service.

This clause emphasises what you value, what your organisation needs to analyse; because without analysis there can be no review and no corrective action.

In my opinion, organisations tend to overlook this part of the standard in many ways, after management review and internal audits have been completed. This is ignored unless an organisation is carrying this out without actually realising it.

Analysis could also be your energy monitoring and efficiencies of organisational processes. You can analyse anything that you want to – just ensure that it is bringing value.

Analysis is also fruitful if you are monitoring your quality goals and objectives. What are these, did you set them correctly and are they helping your organisation perform better? Does everybody know what your organisational objectives are? Communication of these goes a long way.

One matter regarding analysis is trends. Trends are very important for management systems – and negative ones will need identifying. How often have you heard people say in your business "That has happened loads of times and nothing ever gets done"? Well now is your chance to do something about it.

A great way to enquire about analysis is to ask staff what could be done better in the tasks they perform. Only by analysing and discussing information can anything get done about it.

A lot of companies and businesses stagnate. Is this due to analysis? I certainly think so. Looking outward all of the time can deflect your attention to address certain problems or issues inside of an organisation, being too focused can sometimes distort your view of a business.

Many a manager will not improve a process because it may cost too much or the machine that you are using is far too important to stop for scheduled maintenance. Then, when it breaks down, everyone panics. If analysis were carried out in the correct way, plenty of businesses could thrive from this attitude of asking people, analysing the problems, working together and solving it.

Another case in point is being too self focused instead of being focused on the customer. This may lead to lack of discussions with a customer, no customer service, and contract disputes arising from not speaking during contract arrangements. Design problems are a major factor of lack of discussion between two parties and a lack of analytics. Analysis of all of these areas certainly will help your organisation, which is why analysis has been included in this international standard.

However the analysis is totally bespoke. Ensure that you carry this out and use some of my suggestions to help you.

Improvement, continual improvement, corrective action, preventive action

Corrective action and preventive action require a mandatory documented procedure. These are sometimes amalgamated into one procedure at a lot of companies – for the simple reason that the subject is taking action: whether that action is corrective or preventive is just a matter of timing.

For the last part of the standard, we shall talk about the last three clauses together as they are essentially all rolled into one with the slight exception of preventive action, which has to be applied before a problem occurs.

Essentially, improvement and actions are all about being proactive, taking measures to resolve and sorting matters out. So actions and plans are what this part is all about for you. A lot of organisations carry this out, but do not actually write anything down. This causes two problems: (1) sometimes the problem is forgotten and (2) there is no effective plan. The way to get around this quickly is to have an action plan. This should detail the following:

- Date of raising the issue.

- Timeframe for completion and priority level.

- What has occurred or what needs doing to stop something occurring?

- Who is responsible for its completion?

- What are the problems that it may cause?

- Will it cause a non-conformity?

- To what level of non-conformance?

- Details of corrective action and updated plan.

- Were the actions effective? (after a period of weeks / months)

Every action is designed to enable a programme of continual improvement to take place in your organisation.

All data that is collected should be analysed to enable mistakes to be rectified and improvements in all aspects of the business to be made.

The Management Review is a controlled forum for the dissemination of data in order that a controlled programme for improvement can be adopted, so you can include your plans on there. You can 'cut and paste' your plans into the minutes which shows the detail that you have gone to and other staff can have an effective input into this.

The management review is also a great forum for looking at past actions and seeing if they are effective, which is required in the 2008 standard. If the actions are not effective then they should be reviewed. Your organisation should continually improve the effectiveness of the quality management system through the use of all components of the system there to aid this. These are quality goals and policy, internal audits, management reviews, preventive and corrective actions required as a result of this and analysis of your organisation as a whole.

The tools for completing this part of the standard will be in place at this stage, but it is a great idea to include an action planner to record the information. As I mentioned previously, matters are easily forgotten, and a simple, structured plan of improvement is an easy way to satisfy this clause. If you detail faults arising out of internal audits and management reviews on the plan, other people can get to the detail quickly and help bring about a speedy resolution.

A corrective and preventive action procedure should be established and this should provide for:

- Determining potential non-conformities and their causes.

- Documented investigations which identify the (actual and possible) causal factors of procedural or service non-conformance and initiation of action to prevent recurrence.

- Detailed and recorded analysis of processes, operations, concessions, quality records and customer complaints.

- The initiation of identified preventive and corrective action to deal with problems and the implementation of controls to ensure that preventive and corrective actions are effective. (Use your action plan to document this.)

- Recording of changes to established procedures as a result of corrective action.

- Evaluating the need for preventive and corrective action to be taken and reviewing the effectiveness of the actions taken.

All of the actions taken should be commensurate with the level of detail, sophistication and priority level of the organisation. For some, the actions will be swift and cheap; for others they may require detailed analysis, discussion and possible financial input.

As we have discussed previously, in my experience, the only time that a significant investment will be authorised with regards to a non-conformance against the standard is when an organisation seriously needs to upgrade because of possible business repercussions. If non- conformances are standard-related and do not seriously affect the organisational operations, you should choose your requests carefully and not be too forward with requests for finance until you have proven that other avenues have been chosen, unless you really have no alternative.

After word on the clauses

All the clauses that we have discussed are there for your business to dissect and interpret. The standard can be interpreted in many ways: and there are always more than a few avenues to your destination of achieving the ISO 9001 standard.

What I have highlighted to you is the need for certain areas to be addressed and to adopt. My aim is to assist your organisation and to help you to move forward.

Of course, my suggestions will not be applicable in every organisation in every part of the world. However, what I have written will provide benefit to any organisation should you choose to use it, although you do so at your own choosing and risk.

The path that we have discussed will only add value and reduce risk, it will not exacerbate any existing problems or create new ones. As you can see from this book, adding value is what my intentions are about.

My ideas are based on experience and trial and error. I know what works in a wide range of businesses, what helps organisations to prosper and achieve certification.

Heeding the information I have provided may help you to thwart possible repercussions in the future with your customers, suppliers, external auditors or with regulatory requirements.

ISO implementation and certification is a two-way street. The auditors will have their way, you will have yours and the next person will have theirs. The most important piece of advice and information that I can give to you is all about taking action and also listening to others where experience can be gained. You may or may not like what an auditor says to you but they can add value; so keep an open mind when discussing possibilities for improvement.

Take actions and you will succeed. Sometimes, of course, it's necessary to fail before we succeed. But the way in which you respond determines the difference between you and the next person or your organisation from the next one. I am interested in organisations that want to progress, help themselves and be entirely professional at what they do.

My view is to recommend third party accreditation. This is because it is a true sign of business performance when an external professional body audits and examines your organisation to a set standard.

The route is yours to choose, but I recommend third party assessment to a national auditing body. We will discuss certification and your options later in this book.

14. Internal auditing and review

This part of the standard requires a documented procedure, which is mandatory.

Internal auditing can be carried out by anyone in your organisation, preferably impartial from the process or implementation task, but as I highlighted earlier, training is very important to be able to complete this accurately, so we can cover this after we discuss approach. In my opinion, approach is probably the single most important factor in preparing, initiating, completing and reviewing an audit. Approach is the key to gaining information – and that approach should be a well mannered one, from whoever is carrying this out.

It's a sad fact of life that some auditors are cocky, pedantic and think they know more about your business than you do. It doesn't matter how qualified an auditor is; if he is not approachable, professional, trustworthy, friendly and pleasant to deal with, the chances are that you may block his / her efforts in some way. They may also be looking to put things in a negative light.

On the other hand, a good auditor will always be looking for conformance, always be professional, approachable, and firm but fair, and always have an open mind.

Internal auditing and auditing in general is very important to the two parties. Firstly I would like to convey bqmc's code of auditor practice to you for future guidance. This guidance will help you to bear in mind how you may wish to behave as an auditor and gives you an insight into how you should conduct yourself in a fair and professional way.

1. You must act in an honest, unbiased, fit and proper manner. You must show fairness to all involved, to the organisation you are auditing and the one you are representing. You must be polite and courteous at all times.

2. You must disclose any previous relations and business relationships with the organisation that you are about to audit. Before undertaking an audit,

you should be able to demonstrate a fair and decent attitude towards others.

3. You must not accept gifts, profits, money, discounts of products or other items before, during or after undertaking an audit from any party. You have a responsibility to provide an impartial attitude that is to the benefit of all concerned parties.

4. You must not disclose findings or any part of them to those not involved. You must be responsible for the audit team which you may be leading, or of which you are part. You must not knowingly disclose any other information gained in the course of the audit to any third party, unless authorised in writing by the organisation you are auditing.

5. You must not disclose confidential information to third parties who have no right to intervene or request information from you. Audits shall remain confidential and possibly secret, based upon the wishes of the organisation you are auditing. Any request for information on an audit from a third party should be supported by a written letter of authorisation from the organisation that you have audited.

6. You must not act in a biased, prejudiced, racial, discriminatory or inflammatory manner towards the organisation that is being audited or your employer. Be fair, courteous, polite and professional in all of your actions and dealings.

7. You must not act in an unkind way to your employer when auditing a supplier, third party or other. Do not disclose any confidential information which could be a breach of conduct to your employer and result in disciplinary action.

8. If enquiries take place as a result of your audit, your approach should be fair, honest and fully cooperative in achieving the results of this process.

You should not block, alter, hide or erase information that could be important. Your cooperation is paramount and your attitude shall be trustworthy.

9. You must have an open, fair and unbiased manner and approach, audit with precision and not pass judgment until you have exhausted all necessary avenues. Do not audit with a pedantic manner, do not bear malice or disregard others, treat all with respect, fairness and integrity.

10. Smile, be polite and approachable as people can be nervous on audit. However, be firm if required and always be courteous and patient.

As I have described, your approach is everything. You will note that I did not mention training: that's because, although training is highly important, the best auditors can mix this and their experience with a high standard of people skills to get the best out of those being audited.

If you keep that in mind whilst auditing, it will pay you back in 'dividends'. People want to be treated well; and if they are, they will reward you with information that you'll need.

If you have been polite and professional and you are not getting your rewards, the person being audited may be hiding something. That is where your skill comes in, in finding out whether this is the case.

Training

When auditing an organisation, whether your own or that of a contractor or a supplier, you should have to have the correct qualifications to do so. Indeed, the more training that you have had, the better it is for you and for your organisation. Remember, you are there to increase your quality control, not hinder your suppliers. The greater your skill level and experience, the easier you will make it for yourself.

If you are off to audit suppliers, make an appointment, be friendly and build up trust with their quality representatives. Make yourself aware of their characteristics and always ask permission to do anything.

The training for an auditor is split into two main areas: internal auditing for those conducting internal audits and possibly supplier audits; and auditor / lead auditor training.

Internal auditor training will last from two to three days and will consist of a good overview of the standard, how to prepare, carry out and report an audit. You may get an end of course exam and you will receive a certificate.

Auditor / lead auditor training focuses on third party audits and in-depth auditing of suppliers. This is really for professional auditors who carry out audits for certification bodies and / or on their suppliers. The courses usually last up to five days. However, if you are educated to this level, I doubt the auditors should trouble you much on a certification audit, especially if they find out you have the same qualification as they do!

The two levels are a good foundation. I highly recommend the internal auditing course for starters. Then, if you would like further experience and you have a good grasp of the standard, complete the lead auditor course.

On my courses were quite a few people who had not even looked at the ISO 9001 standard. Not surprisingly, they struggled! It really is important to get an excellent grounding in ISO 9001 before you start that course.

Whichever you choose, it could cost between £300 - £1100 depending on who provides the training. Anyone charging more than that would not be offering value for money in my opinion, and I would recommend you look elsewhere. The tutor's experience is what you need, and if you get a good tutor, you will enjoy it. Most tutors I have come across and who taught me have been excellent.

As for implementation training, you can shop around. I find the best training is to get stuck in. There is no better experience. It will save you money if you use someone who has a fair bit of knowledge about an ISO standard. As I said previously, many people will say they have done that, meaning ISO implementation, but it usually is just filling a form out here or there or having been audited in the past.

There is nothing better than asking someone who knows, someone who you can trust, or maybe even a decent consultant.

If you want to choose a consultant to help you, *ISO 10019* provides guidance for the selection of quality management system consultants and the use of their services. It will set you back about £80 – but it could save you a lot of time and effort if you choose the wrong consultant. Or ask the consultant for some references. Even if they consult mainly in another standard, they may still be able to help you as the standards can be quite similar in some instances: this applies more to other standards than ISO 9001. I will have more to say about consultants later in this book.

The internal auditing process can be quite a task. It is your responsibility to check that each area is audited. Sample auditing is the best approach here. That's because you cannot uncover everything and shouldn't try to do so. When auditing, look at a good selection of evidence to give you the most balanced view. If you find something wrong in the first instance, it may be a simple mistake, check a few more examples before you start to think about non-conformities and other issues.

Auditing is about being patient and asking the right questions, it isn't about annoying people. Please remember when internal auditing, if you find something wrong, you may wind people up; some people will not take kindly to your probing questions and being told that something is wrong. I have heard stories of people fainting and even having heart attacks on audit! So, be kind, but firm, when necessary.

Scheduling is of paramount importance. When are you going to carry out your audits? Always ensure you give someone at least a week to prepare. The same goes for an external audit: tell people the auditors are coming in to see you all, put up notices and send emails to all staff.

Do not do as I did once and fail to mention the visit to the MD. My excuse was that he wouldn't be interested as he only cared when it suited him. Unfortunately, this was one of those times that it did suit him.

Give people a plan or a guide to see when they may be audited in the future. A schedule is very important in managing your audits, plus a plan is required by the standard. The best advice I can give is to keep it simple.

You can do one or two things to complete this. On a piece of A4 paper, write down your company processes on the left hand side. Across the top, write the months of the year. Now you can either do the audits all in one month, or depending on your business, spread them out through the year. For more time-consuming processes, this is what I advise. If the processes are pretty simple, you can get it all done and out of the way. Or you could choose to do them twice per year; it really is a matter of choice.

The other way to set out your audits is to write the standard clauses down the left side, keep it to sections 4.2, 4.3 etc, if you write all of the sub clauses down, you could be there forever.

The skill here is to match what the standard requires to your processes. If you know your company well and you know what you are doing, this is a good plan. However, if you are not so sure about what the standard is asking for, you might want to do the processes instead.

Whatever you choose to do, it is a good point to reference your procedures on the audit schedule so that you can see what documents are also applicable to the audit.

When producing your audit programmes it is necessary to ascertain what you are auditing against and where. This may cover:

- The organisation's procedures.
- A standard and the clauses.
- Any other sections tied to the audit?
- The department or section.
- The contract or order.

One common way when working out your programmes is **procedural auditing**. Each procedure of an organisation will be checked and audited to ensure that the processes that have been accepted as best practice are followed. This is easy to do, but if there are lots of procedures it may take a little longer than a process-based audit. It depends on your organisation: again, if you have lots of procedures, split them up or group them, have someone assist you in a department. This type of auditing can be troublesome if you miss out adjoining parts of your systems. Try not to just focus on the procedure; there may be scope for missing something out in between the procedural elements.

Auditing by a clause is an effective way of ensuring that a national or international standard has been reached. It's particularly effective at correcting troublesome parts of a system that an organisation may overlook. It's worthwhile to amalgamate these audits with process audits and use the processes as a further guide for evidence of conformity. By mixing the two you can get the benefits of conforming to your own system as well as an applied standard. Using references from a standard as well as from own your processes is highly beneficial.

Process-based auditing is a very effective way to plan an audit. This is because the audit has no boundary. Following a trail of information and records is a very smart way to see if a project or order is conforming to requirements across many sections in an organisation. The whole process is taken into consideration and the task will involve more than one person in many cases. Before undertaking this audit, the auditor should familiarise themselves with the system or process; the assessment of the input and output is a critical aspect and understanding of it is paramount before starting. A requirement of this type of audit from an internal auditing point of view is that the experience to audit other departments is necessary. In the case of a supplier's organisation, you may have to receive additional training.

If you audit the processes you can start at quoting, then contract review, then planning, then how the company carries its production or service out. Then move on to testing: does it validate or make sure that the product is right? Does the company test and calibrate equipment, does it check goods in / out? Does it have a design stage?

There are so many areas of a business: but in each case, you have to identify what your main processes are, what the important parts are, what could go wrong if something is missed out, and so on. It is a good idea to ask people in these areas what the problems are as you implement, not as you audit. That's because they will be far more open with you and will tell you their problems. If you tell them that they are being audited, they'll know you are taking notes and reporting to someone, so they may be guarded and not inclined to disclose as much.

Get the difficulties out of the way on implementation; because when you are auditing, some people don't see an auditor but a troublemaker. Humans are naturally suspicious, but when you try to help on implementation you will see that they are far more forthcoming. It's worth experimenting with this and seeing what happens.

The schedules are up to you. The external auditor should check up on you when he comes to externally verify your system.

When you uncover non-conformities – and you will, because nobody is perfect – you might want to call them points or actions for improvement. This means the same thing and sounds a lot better!

I recommend that you have an action plan of what to do when you uncover issues. In that plan I would have a responsible person, area where the issue was found, timeframe for completion, and the names of anyone else who needs to be involved. Issues of concern and suggested preventive and corrective actions will be required to ensure that it doesn't happen again.

This action plan is simple to do, so draw one up on excel. I find that if you colour-code your actions, e.g. action not started, action started, partially complete, complete (or words to that effect), it also gives others an idea of what is happening. You could then distribute this around your intranet or on notice boards. I talk about this more in section 8.5 onwards.

Auditing internally can be a fractious business. I have seen people nearly come to blows when suspicions have been raised. Some managers and directors may use them as a tool to catch somebody out when they are not performing. On occasion, I have had a manager come up to me and ask if so and so has done the right job, so watch out. Some people may use your audit as an excuse to verbally reprimand someone. If this is you, beware of what people ask you to do on audit; you could be asked to gain evidence, and if the person who you are auditing gets into trouble as a result of your audit, they may come looking for you for a chat.

If you have someone on audit asking you what a person does, or is doing, be on the look out. If this happens to you, just tell them when you audit you will do all you can to ensure that the business thrives in any area; so if you see a problem you will say so.

If you see a problem with a person, don't get too involved unless it compromises health and safety, raises a product issue or something equally serious. If a person wants information just because they do not like somebody, be careful. Auditing, as you will find out, is not just about bits of information and pieces of paper!

If you are asked about a person's performance it is sometimes better to say you will check to see if their business performance is suitable and report something if it is not. Then you will be able to sit on the fence. In my view, it's always best not to get involved in such things. Remember, you are auditing a system - **not** a person.

Personal liaison

Note: before you read the next section, reciprocation in auditing does not include money or financial gifts. It takes the form of kindness, understanding and decent human nature.

According to sociologists, one of the most widespread and basic forms of human culture is the rule of reciprocation. The rule requires one person to try to repay in kind or gesture, what another person has provided. In the auditor's case, this is in the form of courtesy, listening and helpfulness.

Whilst I do not condone giving gifts and other inducements on audit and never will, my approach on this must not be mistaken nor misinterpreted. An auditor should give with his / her manners and professional approach. Sometimes auditors overlook natural kindness in favour of a more pedantic, harsh approach, which is not beneficial to either party and is not conducive to how an auditor should behave and may lead to obstruction. Some auditors love the power they 'think' that they have.

Giving, in my sense of the word, is by being kind, professional and courteous. The reverse of what I am describing is an auditor who is awkward, always looking to fail you and being belligerent – and there are such people out there.

Auditing techniques and behaviour should use professional and profitable manners. (People should be nice anyway, regardless of auditing.) Most auditors I have come across are great people.

In auditing terms what could you do to get the best out of someone sincerely?

- A friendly gesture such as holding a door open and saying hello to people.
- Addressing staff when necessary on the premises, not ignoring them.
- A compliment to a person about their style or workmanship.
- A compliment on their personal workspace.
- Being approachable as an auditor and listening.
- Approaching negative issues with an open mind.
- Finding out what the person likes about their work.

If you want the best out of people, be interested in them. That's simple human nature. Auditing is not just about facts and figures, it is about getting results by treating the person as a human being and as an individual.

It is right to be aware of some basic human traits if you overstep the line, or, if you press the wrong 'buttons'. You should be aware of people's reactions when auditing: the skill in auditing relies heavily upon a person's ability to communicate clearly and respond well to the person being audited.

Communication is an art that should be at the forefront of auditor training today. 'Remote auditing' – where the auditor does not maintain eye contact, does not have decent communication skills and hides information – can be extremely unnerving.

Auditors should have excellent communication skills; but some can be extremely negative. Why is this so? Because they may be nervous themselves, they may not listen to another point of view for a particular reason. They might be pedantic and picky, looking for faults and non-conformities instead of looking for conformance. They might just lack charisma.

This does not apply to all, just a minority. Please remember though, occasionally auditors are under immense pressure to pass organisations; I have even heard of threats to auditors before now. Auditing is a hard job, so occasionally an auditor may appear negative or have other uncharacteristic traits brought on by stress or worry.

You will know when you meet a negative auditor. They are not happy until they have raised something negative and they seem to dig around in information that they could have moved on from. This seems to be a relic from the past though and is becoming less common.

Always keep this following sentence in mind when auditors come to see you: "Personal emotions, likes and dislikes do not come into the equation as an auditor – they are not in the standard, you are being assessed against fact / the standard".

'Opinion engineering', to coin a phrase, is not welcome. If you (the auditee) know the standard well, you can use it to your advantage and defend yourself from negative auditing. If s/he says they do not like something, say to them "Please tell me where it says 'doesn't like' in the standard" – if you are brave enough! You know your business better than most. If you are a person who has taken care over your management system, like I and my customers do, defend your work where appropriate. Stay calm and do not go 'up the wall!'

The professional auditor will seek other routes of compliance before issuing judgement on your work. Remember auditors, internal and external are there to add value, or should be.

Negative auditing can be quite unpleasant. I have seen even strong-minded people become a terrible mess. I always stick up for clients on audit, but you cannot control what a person is feeling. So, if you are an auditor, be aware of people's feelings, respect them and be nice. Keep the following in the back of your mind:

What are the signs of an auditee becoming stressed?

- Reddening of the face.
- Quick speech and unrecognised words.
- Scrambled information.
- An aggressive attitude or defensiveness
- Blank responses.
- Shifty movements.
- Uncharacteristic voice pitch.
- Raised or crossed arms.
- Sweaty palms when greeting.
- Denial or 'passing of the buck'.
- Anxiety and excuses.

What can you do when you witness this?

- Be polite and courteous (as always).
- Draw their attention to excellent workmanship.
- Give them positive encouragement to focus on.
- Ask if they have a co-worker who can assist?
- Have a toilet break.
- Be aware of the need for diplomacy.
- If it is not that serious in your opinion, do not raise a problem or non-conformity.
- Tell them you can see the hard effort that they have gone to.

- Remember, auditing is about sampling pieces of work, not interrogation on every matter. If you have enough information to satisfy yourself, do not overdo it.
- Leave the auditee alone and move on. It is not the end of the world if you do not get every last detail.

When auditing you will see people in all sorts of situations. Some like to talk a lot and you cannot get a word in. Then there are quiet people who will only speak when they are spoken to, there are people who will tell you all of their family problems and who they do not like at work. There will be the person that doesn't care that you are there at all, there will be others who will address you politely and think you are a godly being. There are also the sensible ones who take the problems at face value and try and change their company for the better.

There are literally millions of personalities to come across. Managing this is a very big task: and as I have mentioned previously, people management is what auditing is all about. It does not matter what type of person they are, the question is: can you get the most out of them as an individual and can you get them to respond to your requests? If you can do that with most people you are 90 per cent there. The training, experience and the correct questions will do the rest.

Ask them how they are. Are they having a good day? What are they currently working on, is it interesting? Etc. Of course this should all be used as a short introduction. Some people don't respond well to this but most want to be listened to and liked, so asking them about themselves before you delve into their work is both polite and reassuring. Going straight for the jugular with loaded questions is something an interrogator would do. If you are too quick on the draw with the person you're auditing, it shouldn't surprise you if they think of you more as a prosecutor than a helper.

It is all about talking to a person. They are not robots and neither are you. Speaking to human beings in the right way will get you the results you desire and a reputation of being a fine auditor: if you can couple that with the professional skills that an auditor requires to do his or her job correctly.

Impartiality

When auditing, you or whoever is completing this audit should be impartial to the process or department. But you must have a knowledge of what goes on in it. If you have set up and implemented the management system, then get someone else in to audit you on that.

When I was a quality manager I used to get a friend of mine to come in and do the audits of the management system because I had set it up and implemented it. His name is Paul Plumridge of QuServe, a really nice guy and a great ambassador to auditors and consultants. If you live in the Midlands and need assistance with your audits or system, look Paul up at his website (http://www.qu-serve.co.uk/) and tell him I said to give him a call.

ISO 9001 also points you to another standard, *ISO 19011, guidelines for quality and / or environmental management systems auditing.*

I like these helpful documents, but they come at a cost, so check out your budget. The main standard you should focus on is the one you are implementing; that said however, ISO 14004 is a great guide for ISO 14001 implementation likewise BS OHSAS 18002 for BS OHSAS 18001 implementation. They are better than the actual standards themselves in my opinion, because they also give great guidance.

People say to me that sometimes there is far too much technical jargon in standards (which is necessary I am afraid), and wanting to unravel the jargon led me to write this book.

The ISO 9000 and ISO 14000 series of International Standards emphasise the importance of audits as a management tool for monitoring and verifying the effective implementation and auditing of an organisation's quality and/or environmental management systems.

ISO 19011 is an international standard that sets guidelines for:

- quality management systems auditing

- environmental management systems auditing

It has been developed to act as a guideline for auditing and is particularly useful, especially if this is your first go at auditing. It's quite reasonable at around £80.00 but can be effective and gives you some very useful tips.

The standard offers four resources to organisations to aid you in your advancement. It helps to give:

- An explanation of the principles of management systems auditing.

- Guidance on the management of audit programmes and activities.

- Guidance on the conduct of internal and external audits.

- Advice on the competence and evaluation of suitable auditors.

Audits are an essential part of standards and conformity assessment activities: and as we have discussed, the standard can certainly help you to choose the right path.

ISO 19011 provides guidance on the management of audit programmes, the conduct of internal or external audits of quality and / or environmental management systems, as well as on the competence and evaluation of auditors.

It is intended to apply to a broad range of potential users, including auditors, organisations implementing quality and/or environmental management systems, organisations needing to conduct audits of quality and/or environmental management systems for contractual reasons, and organisations involved in auditor certification or training and certification.

The clauses starting with 4 describe the principles of auditing. These principles help the user to appreciate the essential nature of auditing and they are a necessary prelude to clauses 5, 6 and 7.

Clause 5 provides guidance on managing audit programmes and covers such issues as assigning responsibility for managing audit programmes, establishing the audit programme objectives, coordinating auditing activities and providing sufficient audit team resources.

Clause 6 provides guidance on conducting audits of quality and/or environmental management systems, including the selection of audit teams. Or audit members. Clause 7 provides guidance on the competence needed by an auditor and describes a process for evaluating auditors.

Where quality and environmental management systems are implemented together, it is at the discretion of the user as to whether the quality management system and environmental management system audits are conducted separately or together.

My personal view on this is simple: keep them separate. People amalgamate them for ease of use, but for me, each item in your company is separate – especially health and safety standards. That should really be undertaken by an experienced health and safety officer. It is right to amalgamate the documentation so that it is all locatable and controlled from one management point, but manuals and procedures should be separate in my opinion. I have seen some great amalgamated systems, though; it is purely down to choice.

Although ISO 19011 is applicable to the auditing of quality and environmental management systems, you can consider adapting or extending the guidance to apply to other types of audits, including other management system audits, like occupational health and safety (BS OHSAS 18001) or information security (ISO / IEC 27001).

The ISO 19011 standard is there to offer guidance on auditing. It is a great document; if you have received training from a company like WCS, BQMC, BSI, Isoqar, LRQA, Moody International or NQA, they may use it in their training packages.

Performing an audit

Opening meeting

An internal audit does not usually have an opening meeting as such, but it is best to see how one works, in case you need to be involved in one or have to plan one as part of a supplier audit. However, there is no reason why you cannot have a mini opening meeting with each department or auditee; indeed, it is good practice.

When conducting or attending an opening meeting, it is important to look at the human element of auditing and the perception of auditors. Following on from previous sections, using practical and theoretical techniques, we can greatly influence the auditee with our approach and significantly affect the outcome by being professional and diligent throughout.

We previously discussed and practised all of the elements to approaching an internal audit; we have prepared our checklists; and are now ready to carry out the audit.

We should brief the management/directors to inform them of how the audits may proceed throughout the year. The lead auditor would carry this out on a formal certification audit or supplier audit; they may have their representatives with them and will be attended by representatives of the organisation they are auditing.

The opening meeting is usually carried out with the Management Representative (minimum) and they are usually accompanied by a director. It is sometimes useful to have audit guides or other managers present, but is important that a senior figure understands this.

The meeting will be chaired by the lead auditor and usually takes from 15 to 30 minutes depending on the size of the organisation. Inform the attendees of how the audit is going to pan out throughout the day and who will be required at certain points. The plan of the audit will be given to the senior management and any issues shall be discussed at this point.

What will be discussed?

- Introduction and confidentiality.
- Scope of audit and exclusions if necessary.
- Availability of personnel and guides.
- Audit plan and locations.
- Raising potential non-conformities.
- Health and safety points.
- Reporting issues, questions and further actions.
- If a certification audit, closing meeting time and location.

As an internal auditor, you may not be required to do this but it is very good practice to ensure that your auditee and guide know how you are planning to proceed.

Introductions are necessary if people do not know each other, it is common courtesy and people are generally more responsive when addressed correctly. Sometimes a private office or room may be requested for the audit staff, depending on availability and location.

Confidentiality of the audit should be discussed. The auditee should be at ease that what you discuss will not be divulged to anybody else apart from the audit team and the senior management. This is important: if the auditee feels they cannot trust you, they may be unwilling to reveal information.

Scope of the audit is concerning what the boundaries of that audit are and if any standards are being audited against, what buildings or offices may be concerned, and if there are any exclusions when auditing to ISO 9001.

Availability of personnel and guides is important on audit. You will need access to people and areas. Ensuring that people are available at particular times is of paramount importance.

Audit plans and locations are to be discussed so that people are aware of where you may be, who you will be with and to ensure that available staff will be in attendance. Audit plans show the auditee your aims; any rearrangement can be discussed.

Raising potential non-conformities should be addressed to put people at ease as to how the process works. Non-conformities are to be used as a tool for progress, not for bullying someone into action or 'telling tales' on people.

The raising of **health and safety** points is to be addressed so that you are aware of any potential dangers or concerns. Highlighting risks and dangerous areas should be included here, as well as fire safety precautions and evacuations. (Are there any fire drills scheduled for that day?)

Reporting issues, questions and further actions is to be conveyed to the auditee and team. This is to ensure that a good dialogue takes place between the two parties. Any concerns or questions about the audit from the auditee should be addressed here.

On a certification audit or supplier audit, a **closing meeting** shall be performed to highlight any issues or concerns and to mention positive points that came out of the audit. If there are problems early on in the audit, these should be conveyed at the time; there should be no surprises at the closing meeting.

Asking questions and communication

As we have discussed previously, your approach is very important. Desirable qualities for an auditor to have are as follows:

- Good communication skills.
- Fair and polite.
- Professional.
- Firm when appropriate.
- Focused and not distracted easily.
- Logical thinking.
- Diplomatic.
- Open minded and willing to listen.
- Well mannered.
- Punctual.
- Well dressed.

Undesirable qualities can severely affect an audit, harm your organisation's reputation and damage your own standing as an auditor. These could include:

- Aggression.
- Rudeness.
- Lateness.
- Scruffy appearance.
- Testing a person and putting them under sustained pressure, silences etc.
- Not listening and appearing uninterested.
- Displaying arrogance and 'know it all' characteristics.
- Ignorance of others.
- Picky and pedantic; always looking for a problem.
- Butting in.

It is very important that you display excellent communication skills on audits. Effective ways to discuss matters are integral to the success and planning of your operation. There are many activities when auditing that we take for granted; the skill set required will involve some or all of the following:

- Asking questions and listening to answers.
- Taking notes (positive and negative).
- Testing the systems of work.
- Sampling documents and records.
- Verifying evidence.
- Seeking objective evidence.
- Following a paperwork trail (audit trail).
- Keeping the auditee informed and discuss matters logically.

Make sure that the auditee understands what you are asking or requesting. Do they appear at ease or show signs of misgivings? Pressure in an auditing situation is not always apparent: easy questions can sometimes fluster people. Possibilities for misunderstanding can be quite common, and people will often say to you, 'I do not understand' or 'What do you mean?' If there are language barriers too, that could lead to further difficulties.

It's important to clarify. If you see that the person being audited is stalling, ask 'Are you okay with the question?' or 'Do you understand what I am asking?'

A number of key points to remember when asking your questions:

- Think before you ask the question – do *you* understand the process?
- Keep questions straightforward; do not overcomplicate or use jargon.
- Do not try to catch the auditee out or have hidden agendas.
- Speak clearly.
- Be positive.
- Encourage.

- Do not jump to conclusions or raise unnecessary non-conformities.

When **asking questions** it is very important that we think first; you cannot erase what you have said. When on audit, we are there to gather information, not to interrogate or coerce.

When conversing on audit, there should be a balance. The auditor should speak for only around 20 to 25 per cent of the time: the rest of the conversation should be carried by the auditee. They should be able to answer the questions well, but you may find that you need to offer help.

The following types of information may be considered when trying to get different levels of information from an auditee:

- Open - to get information from the respondent.
- Closed - to get confirmation of a subject or matter.
- Multiple - could be causing confusion. Should be used when explaining in order to highlight a matter, not for questioning an auditee.
- Rhetorical - not wanting an answer when clarifying something out loud.
- Leading - can be misleading or biased to a topic.

Open questions are by far the most common. They will be used most of the time so that the auditor can understand the processes etc. They invite the auditee to provide input.

Open questions could be:

1. How do you do this?
2. What procedures do you follow?
3. What is the nature of your training?

If you use: what, why, when, who, where and how, you will be able to use open answers to get most of your information.

Closed questions could be:

1. Is this your work instruction here?
2. Is that the finished product?
3. Have these items been tested?

When asking questions with a quick answer, be aware that you may need to ask more open questions in order to re-establish what you are seeking.

Using **multiple questions can** lead to problems. You may stifle the auditees thinking or upset them, so be wary of this approach. Examples could be:

1. What is the date on that drawing, who signed it off, are they authorised to do so, who checked it before it was accepted?

    Or

2. Who was carrying out that job, what were they doing, are they qualified, do they have a work instruction, are they around?

Multiple questions should only be used in a **rhetorical** fashion i.e. when talking to yourself out loud when clarifying a point to yourself - not to the auditee. The auditee then has the opportunity to put you right if you do not fully understand what was said to you.

An instance of this could be if you are reading a work instruction and it has questions aimed at the operator (auditee):

1. Have you set the correct temperature?
2. What is the speed of the feed?
3. Is it correctly set for that product?

Listening

As an auditor, listening is an invaluable skill to develop. When people convey information to you, listen with great attention and look them in the eye. Listening takes a lot of concentration and effort, but it will be worth it: an auditee that sees that you are listening will be much more open and honest with you.

The process of listening should be interactive between the parties. From the auditor's point of view this may include:

1. Clarification of the points.
2. Confirmation of the information.
3. Responding and checking.
4. Acknowledgement.
5. Summarising any points.

By carrying out a mixture of the above, you will reflect back to the auditee that you are listening and place great interest on what s/he says. A person who feels valued will like you more and will be keen to give you the correct information.

Of course, the auditor should be silent when listening and display eye-to-eye contact. Note though that neither the silence nor the eye-contact should be over-extended, as these approaches place stress on the auditee.

When auditing, pauses whilst you are taking notes are necessary; but when you look up again, you should be ready with more questions unless you have the information that you require. In this case, do not leave it too long or the auditee may become anxious – they are also likely to have work to do and may feel that you are holding them up. I always ask if it is okay for me to take notes whilst they talk, so they know that I am not being rude by doing something else, if you do not take notes, you may miss valuable information on a summary.

Sometimes, pauses and silences will be filled with unwanted information by a nervous auditee. They may feel obliged to let you know about other matters, which sometimes lead to non- conformance! At other times, it may be just trivial talk. You may need to stem the flow of this with a quick question – if you can get a word in.

The auditor should not be stalled or distracted. Concentrating on what the auditee has to say will stop your attention from being selective, prejudiced or emotional. Your personal thoughts may get in the way and you might not like what the auditee is saying, but your responses should be rational and unbiased.

Verifying

When listening to questions, verifying the answers requires that you do not mishear or misinterpret what the auditee is saying. Gathering factual information is of prime importance and ensures that you understand the message that they are trying to get across to you.

Asking auditees to 'show you' the process or other information regarding your questions is sometimes the only way of gathering factual objective evidence. This can lead to somebody thinking that you may not believe what they are saying. Following a natural route that leads effortlessly to the final answers is a good way of achieving information without being too invasive.

Asking 'how does this work?' or 'could you just show me the procedure, please?' will lead the auditee to think that this is just a natural progression. If you are questioning the validity of something, take a mental note of it and ask to see it later on in the audit. You can always go back to an area for clarification.

The auditee should not feel under any pressure; however, this is sometimes hard to avoid. Some people are prone to nervousness and will need more than your usual calming tactics to feel at ease. Unfortunately, most auditees do display signs of nervousness.

Once you have understood the evidence, it is important to be aware of how deeply you need to check. Sampling is a good idea. If you are sampling records, it is important to look at more than one; your sample should be well balanced and show a fair reflection of their system. So if there were ten procedures, you might scrutinise three of four: if there were a hundred personnel, you could check 10-15 training records, and so on. If there were hundreds of thousands of products, you might want to request further records, customer complaints and returns for evidence of conformance.

If you encounter a problem when sampling, it is best to check some more of the same to find out if it is an isolated case or something that is deeply embedded. By then refining your verification, you can usually achieve the good results you are seeking on audit. If the findings are negative, you can refine the message you are trying to pass to the organisation and get them to understand the nature of any issue.

Effective note-taking

During the audit there is a requirement for effective note-taking. This is about recording evidence that is clear, precise, legible and traceable back to the department, subject, process or person, and might involve interpreting a process in your own words. For example, note-taking about purchasing might go something like this:

- Ask for permission to order.
- Get order number or purchase number.
- Contact supplier.
- Take references.
- Date of delivery.
- Who is to be contacted – notes to goods in.
- Contact accounts/put on accounting package.
- Inform staff when arrival is expected.
- Delivery notes.

Note-taking when auditing a process should follow a logical structure. For instance:

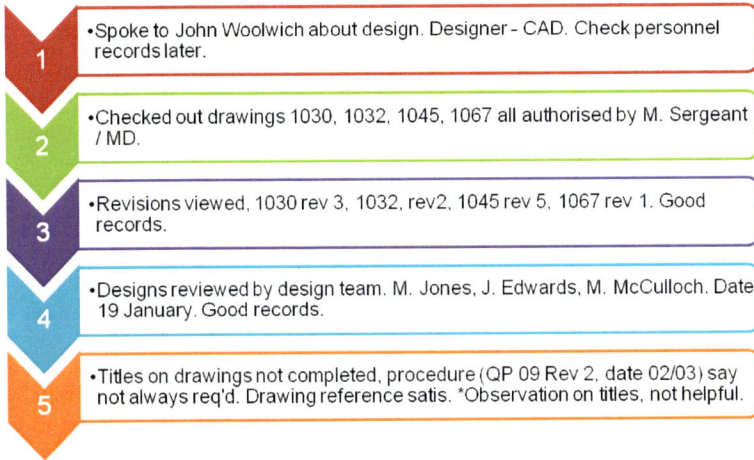

1. •Spoke to John Woolwich about design. Designer - CAD. Check personnel records later.

2. •Checked out drawings 1030, 1032, 1045, 1067 all authorised by M. Sergeant / MD.

3. •Revisions viewed, 1030 rev 3, 1032, rev2, 1045 rev 5, 1067 rev 1. Good records.

4. •Designs reviewed by design team. M. Jones, J. Edwards, M. McCulloch. Date 19 January. Good records.

5. •Titles on drawings not completed, procedure (QP 09 Rev 2, date 02/03) say not always req'd. Drawing reference satis. *Observation on titles, not helpful.

This effective-note taking will help you to arrive at your conclusions at the end of your reporting. It will help you to clarify and provide consistent value at a time of audit that may be scrutinised and argued upon. If you have decent notes and evidence, you will be able to argue your case if required.

It can be difficult at first, but taking this approach can help you to understand a process. You can make your own drawings and sketches to help you; and the best way when you are starting to audit is ask the auditee to explain the process to you in simple terms so that you can write it down.

It is sometimes necessary to ask the auditee if you can take notes while they are speaking, so that they know you are not being disrespectful when not maintaining eye contact. Copies and photocopies can become burdensome, but writing down the information that you require and understand can help you to quickly gauge what you need and what is relevant.

Teamwork

Teamwork is everything in an organisation. Of course, audits are sometimes done by individuals and by a team. When groups of auditors work together, it is important to ensure that they are consistent and do not contradict each other – especially in front of the client. The lead auditor should have regular contact with the rest of the audit team and monitor progress.

It is essential that the team meet together, away from the auditee and the organisation, and discuss matters properly and professionally.

A team should be strong, be led by an experienced member and listen to each person's inputs. All information should be valued.

Summary of performing an audit

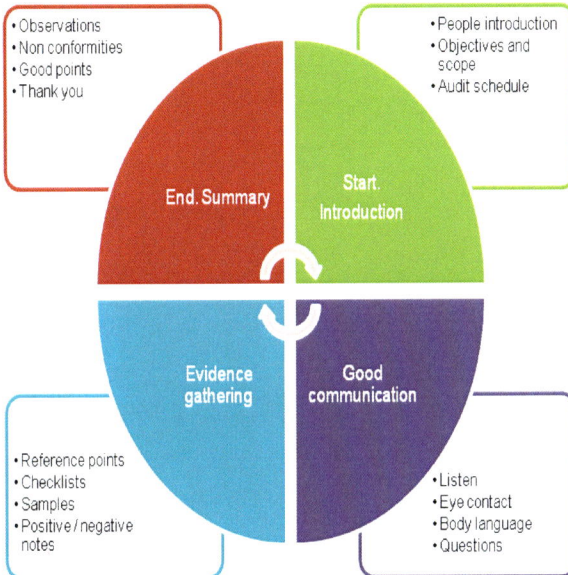

- Observations
- Non conformities
- Good points
- Thank you

- People introduction
- Objectives and scope
- Audit schedule

End. Summary

Start. Introduction

Evidence gathering

Good communication

- Reference points
- Checklists
- Samples
- Positive / negative notes

- Listen
- Eye contact
- Body language
- Questions

15. Problems encountered – and why organisations may not pass their audit first time?

There are many reasons why organisations do not pass their first audits when going for ISO certification: some of these are common, others less so.

First, we need to identify what reasons the certification bodies give when your certificate is being put on hold. These could include:

- A major element of the standard is missing from the implementation project. This can be called a **critical** or **major** non-conformity. It could result in a re-audit and involve substantial additions or changes that will have to be checked again either off-site or onsite.

- Minor faults that constitute a reason not to provide the certificate to the organisation until the problems have been fixed or procedures are in place to fix them. These are called **minors or opportunities for improvement**. This will require some additional work, the time of which will vary depending on the issue(s).

Overall, if you are good enough, you pass, if you are not, the certificate will be put on hold until you display the correct requirements.

It really comes down to the auditor on the day: if he/she thinks that you are good enough, then his/her professional view counts, full stop. If he/she decides to overlook matters because you have entered into the spirit of the standard and the mistake is easily rectified, sometimes a decision needs to be made and the effort rewarded. However, I must stress that this should only be the case where the effort has been put in, if the mistake is simple to rectify and it can be done on the day of the audit. I cannot condone passing an organisation if they do not deserve it.

Although not on my auditing or consultancy watch, I have known businesses with the flimsiest quality management systems pass. I have also known in-depth QMS's and highly professional staff fail because of one reason or another.

My attitude is that if auditors give you non-conformities, listen to what they say. Many a non-conformity has value behind it that you can build on: as the old saying goes, experts are people who have learned from their mistakes. Negative auditing and non-conformities should only be challenged if you think that the auditor is treating you unjustly and you can back up this belief.

When I am auditing, if something isn't good enough, I say so; and then it's their job to put it right. The standard has to be earned in all respects. If an auditor overlooks something that he should not have, and you have a problem with your customers because it has been ignored, overlooking the problem may end up causing you more concerns. Turning a blind eye doesn't add value.

In most cases organisations deserve to pass their accreditation, simply through sheer effort. Nevertheless, it can be a difficult task passing first time when it is a large organisation with lots of people and masses of information to digest and disseminate.

So why do organisations have difficulties passing their audits? One of the most common reasons is that something is missing on implementation: they have either not read the standard properly or have missed a procedure out. What is missing can vary, of course; but it is usually the case that the standard has been incorrectly interpreted somewhere.

I can understand that, to some people, the standard can seem complicated, difficult to understand and talk in a 'language' that is sometimes difficult to penetrate. As I have previously mentioned, the languages that the standard has to be translated to must be commensurate and mean the same thing worldwide. I think that the ISO has got it right; but a lot of staff I speak to do not understand the standard. It all comes down to usage and being familiar with it.

There are other reasons for failing. One common explanation is that people overlook safety concerns. We are not there to audit health and safety but if it concerns your infrastructure – which is in the standard – your certificate can be withheld until you prove that you have taken effective corrective action.

Another reason is that technical procedures have been overlooked on a product or service. If you manufacture pressurised steel pipes and you do not have your equipment calibrated to national standards, which could contravene build standards? The pipe could eventually crack and someone could be seriously injured. If you do not calibrate your machinery and test your staff, you could be looking at difficulties on audit: in which case the certificate could be withheld until you have your machinery calibrated and your staff correctly tested by a third party body.

Electrical testing is another area to be aware of. If your products are electrical and you do not test them, will you pass? It's doubtful, to say the least.

If you are mechanical engineers and you have no staff experience logged or educational certificates for them, your accreditation may again be delayed.

If your quality policy is missing, or if it does not say what it needs to say, and you have no commitment from senior management, this could also constitute a problem – albeit one that is easy to sort out.

When you purchase your supplies, if you do not check them at goods inward, that may be regarded as having no quality control, which again could contravene the standard in the product realization section, especially if you really do need some form of control.

The best advice I can give to you is to read the standard three times. Each time please highlight on the standard what is missing or what is necessary, put question marks against what you do not understand, note down any worries, ask professional assistance, ask for advice: and never ignore what you do not understand.

Some of my clients call me and spill their worries. It sometimes takes me a minute to explain, sometimes five minutes: but at the end of the conversation, they will be happy and have no further need to worry because I put them at ease about it. So if you don't understand anything, get it sorted out. That way your implementation will be quicker.

A great deal of minor issues come from lack of revision control, paperwork all over the place and not suitably controlled. In my opinion if you control your paperwork from one electronic file, branching into other files for each department, this is easy to stay on top of.

Get people to give their input, uncover those hidden forms and have one place to control them from. Standardisation of document control and control of documentation is a common way to fall down on audit. If you control it well, this should be easy on audit. Conversely, a loose or uncontrolled area is likely to throw up several indiscretions that the audit will uncover, mainly through lack of revision control.

When an auditor gives you a non-conformity/opportunity for improvement, take any advice offered and implement what is missing. Most of the time, it will not take long. And as I suggested, many non-conformities can help a business to become more effective.

Remember that the auditor is there to audit you, not to provide consultancy. I think a lot of auditors will give you an idea of what is needed informally, but in reality when we are auditing we should not give helpful assistance on your systems; that is governed by the rules and regulations that we abide by. Impartiality agreements and auditor codes of practice dictate what we can and cannot do as an auditor when working on the behalf of an accreditation/certification body. If we audit you, we are not allowed to consult with you in a separate arrangement, usually for two to three years depending on the accreditation body. That is not to say that an auditor will just shun your request for additional information; there's always the opportunity to ask for extra clarification of what the auditor is saying.

Common sense and decency is the correct approach. The worst case I have seen where the client said "I don't understand that non-conformity", and the auditor's response was "I am sorry but I am not here to consult, it is black and white to me." – unprofessional and robotic.

If some auditing companies knew how some of their auditors behaved, causing people to switch certification bodies just to rid themselves of a particular auditor, they would hit the roof. I do not influence my clients on this too much, it is an organisational choice; but if the auditor oversteps the mark, then I have my say. Personal skills and communication are not focused on enough on audit training. 'Little despots' dishing out non-conformances at will are damaging to a certification body's business if they are not agreed with or understood by the organisation being audited. Some companies are afraid of their auditors, and that cannot be right.

I have digressed a little here: but I wanted to make sure that if you encounter a problem, you know you can request extra details within the boundaries of the audit. Of course this won't result in masses of detail, but asking for additional information from their point of view does nobody any harm – and will probably do lots of good. After all, most auditors have lots of valuable experience, so why get the benefit of that when given the opportunity?

Good auditors will 'play the game'. They'll get to know you, they will have a keen eye for what is right, they use common sense effectively and know when to take matters as they see them. They will have a good sense of direction, be quick to notice problems but lend a sensible ear when things are not quite right. They will talk to you like a human being, be gracious and accepting, be quick to dismantle worries and anxieties and use their calm influence to get the best out of the auditee without placing undue amounts of stress on them. Such auditors will always be welcomed: because they understand how things work and they understand that businesses do not always run perfectly.

Being helpful and knowledgeable makes us human, makes us pleasant to deal with – and makes us professional. We must remember that in practice, seldom is anything what it is meant to be on paper or in a regulation. You cannot always go by what is written down: business life is not set in tablets of stone.

Private organisations and staff may have spent months or sometimes years implementing these management systems. They do not want some 'stuffy' auditor who will not clarify their non-conformity. I have seen this a few times, I sometimes think that auditors raise non-conformities and then regret them because they cannot back them up when challenged. And there is the flip side, when a non conformance should be raised and then it is not.

The saying 'don't bite the hand that feeds you' applies to this industry just as much as it does to any other. If an auditor gives you an idea what he wants to see in future, it doesn't hurt anybody to hear it. Explain your non-conformities clearly.

The main reason organisations fall down on audit is mostly down to a lack of knowledge about the standard, or, If the system is not being taken seriously and is not conjoined with your everyday workings, it can be difficult to get through first time.

In my experience, those that try, pass: and those that carry this out for a marketing exercise have trouble with the system, usually after passing, because once they have the tick in the box, they are not so worried about it anymore. Some organisations think that it is a paperwork exercise and don't realise what's hit them come the main audit when all processes are thoroughly scrutinised.

Remember, a management system *is* your business, not some computer programme or pieces of flimsy documentation just covering the basics of the standard. Thoroughness is the key here.

16. Amalgamation with other standards

Amalgamation of standards is becoming increasingly common throughout the world: and the ISO is trying hard to make this easier for the implementer.

I think that this approach is very welcome, because a lot of organisations are taking the integrated approach. Whether you agree on this or not, you have to applaud the ISO for listening and adapting to what is asked for.

Of course, amalgamation does a number of things. It conjoins procedures, it gives a baseline format to use and understand, and it gives a control point for all of the standards in an organisation.

This helps a business to combine its efforts in many important sectors. Information security (ISO 27001), quality (ISO 9001), environmental (ISO 14001) and health and safety (BS OHSAS 18001), can all join together to enable an organisation to run smoothly and effectively. I concentrate on these four standards as they are among the most popular and well known in my business circles.

For a beginner, it can be difficult when faced with such an implementation task. If I were starting from scratch, I would do ISO 9001 first, get certified and understand the process of certification: then add ISO 14001 and any others to suit. If you wanted to add 14001 and 18001, this could be carried out simultaneously because of their likeness in the written form.

I must stress however that ISO 14004 and BS OHSAS 18002 – the two documents that give general guidelines, principles to follow and great insight into their common standards – are a world apart because of what they are to be used for: environmental and occupational health and safety guidelines respectively.

Amalgamation works fine, if you take each step at a time. Work on each one in turn and gradually amalgamate the systems together: that's a sensible approach.

A lot of certification bodies are increasingly showing an appetite for joint auditing of these standards. I feel that this approach can squeeze people into not giving the full attention to each standard – which they deserve.

The ISO may move away with their promotion of integrated management systems eventually? Not only will these systems grow, but the focus on individual items and their quality of delivery, such as environmental or health and safety management, may suffer for some. That seems inevitable to me. If you are concentrating on two standards at a time, how can you give your full attention to either? I think these integrated systems are a good idea in principle but eventually they may fade away?

Some people I come across implement ISO 9001, and then their manager will say, "Oh why don't you do '18001' as well now?" The two are a world apart in practice and I have seen many an implementer become bogged down with extra standards. Someone who is a quality manager with no health and safety experience should not be implementing BS OHSAS 18001 on their own, no way. If they have the experience, then that is fine.

Eventually the certification bodies may recognise that joint approaches actually earn them less money and prove to have far greater complications when trying either to recruit auditors or get the best out of training. Everybody has to be dual-skilled. Well, as other areas of life prove, dual skills do not always deliver quality.

If you are of the same opinion as me, you will prefer not to see the occupational health and safety standard (BS OHSAS 18001) combined with anything, with the exception of the environmental standard (ISO 14001) if you really have to.

The reason I say this is that they are both highly concerned with taking care of your staff, organisation, concerns and legislation at all levels, and at the time of writing they are extremely similar in their design. However, I see health and safety as an absolute priority in any organisation and take the opinion that it should be managed apart from everything else by a dedicated team and system of work.

219

Let me explain. Mismanagement of quality can get you a telling off or the sack. Mismanagement of environmental management may get you the sack and/or a fine from the authorities, and possibly legal action. Mismanagement of information security could get you the same; people can also be jailed for unwanted information disclosure if it gets onto the wrong hands and abused.

However, mismanagement of health and safety can send you straight to prison if fatalities or extremely serious cases are involved. You could lose your business and your reputation, not to mention the injuries or fatalities on your conscience and the vicious comebacks if you have not upheld your duty of care to others.

There is a world of difference in accountability and responsibility here. That's why accountability is used in the 18001 standard, and not in the other three as yet.

The British Standard Occupational Health and Safety Assessment Series (BS OHSAS 18001), assists you in the professional management of your company occupational health and safety systems. I regard this standard as one that improves staff safety the most of course, as well as the general health, safety and infrastructure of your organisation as a whole. It should be managed by a health and safety officer or someone else who knows health and safety well.

This standard is about looking after your staff and their health – a vital area. I do not think attentions should be drawn away from this standard by amalgamation with ISO 9001, ISO 27001 or others. To me, health and safety is such an important issue, and it should receive the undivided attention it deserves. I also wouldn't like to explain to a Judge (if something went disastrously wrong) that you implemented a few standards together because if 'was easier to'.

That is not to say that I have not been requested to amalgamate it with other standards, I have done and will do if requested, but I would not in my own organisation. I think it wholly right to use BS OHSAS 18001, and to control it separately for full focus.

If I had to choose a standard to amalgamate it with, it would be ISO 14001 - Environmental Management Systems. At the time of writing, the two standards are compatible, very similar apart from one or two clauses and have been deliberately formatted to assist the user, which is a good thing.

The four standards that I consult on are all familiar to each other, and the documentation control and procedures can usually be amalgamated.

Integration of standards is a choice for the organisation. At bqmc we have a joint quality and environmental management system. These standards are, in my opinion, two of the most compatible and it is straightforward to integrate the ISO 14001 standard into your existing quality management system.

If I were to add the health and safety system, I would only control the health and safety documents from a quality control perspective. The system after that would be entirely separate and the person carrying this out would not be facilitating my quality and environmental management at the same time. At the end of the day, it is your choice.

Part 3: Certification / accreditation

17. The scope of your organisation for certification

What is your business scope?

Scopes of businesses or organisations apply directly to your certificate. Certification bodies like to see simplified scopes on application that relate directly to what your organisation does. For instance, if you were a civil engineering contractor, your scope might read:

"We specialise in the supply of civil engineering contracting."

This is the certification body's signal and opportunity to send an auditor who is familiar with your sector, rather than sending someone whose competence is in gardening. You may laugh; but there is a valid reason for this. When an organisation is being audited, the person completing the assessment on behalf of the certification body should have appropriate competence in your area, so that he or she can understand your processes and have a good idea of whether you suit the requirements of a standard or not.

This also stops you as an organisation 'pulling the wool over their eyes' and fooling them with nonsense. It happens. So beware, when your auditor comes along to see you, he or she may know more about your product, services and systems than you do. That is why the scope is important.

Scopes of business serve other purposes. They really do help the certification body, and they will usually ask you to tell them what their scope is at the start of the process.

Alongside this request they will probably ask you how many sites you have and how many people work for your company at each site. The certification body needs to assess how long it will take them to complete the process for your organisation, which can vary wildly of course. It all depends on the organisation, where you operate and what you do. The certification body will then judge what is required against its instructions from the national body, which guides certification bodies on how many days that they require, depending on the organisation.

It also allows the certification body to place your scope of accreditation on the certificate, so if you are a civil engineering contractor and you decide to try your hand at fencing for the sake of a business opportunity, you may not be accredited for that part of your business until:

1. You inform the certification body; and

2. You are audited against extra requirements, relating to your venture.

This also stops an organisation from proclaiming that they are ISO 9001 accredited in everything that they do, if they are not.

If you are unsure of a supplier, ask them for their certificate if they have one to see their scope of accreditation.

Scope of certification with reference to clause 7 (See also section 7).

If you did not know already, you can exclude your company from certain parts of ISO 9001. If you look in the standard on clause 1.2, it will tell you that this **only** applies to clause 7. Product realization.

Product realization contains various information and instructions on what you must do to conform to requirements on:

- Planning.
- Determining and reviewing requirements.
- Customer communication.
- Design and development.
- Purchasing.
- Control of your service/product.

- Validation of processes (testing or checks to ensure they meet planned requirements).
- Identification and traceability.
- Customer property.
- Preservation of (your and your customers') product.
- Control of monitoring and measuring equipment.

The above information is designed so that if your organisation does not carry out a particular clause operationally, then it can be excluded from it.

For instance with 7.3 design and development, a company can exclude itself from being audited against this clause if it does not design its own products or services. The company then has a genuine reason for not carrying out clause 7.3 in their management system and it will be excluded from the audit scope – if the auditor agrees.

However, you cannot absolve yourselves from responsibility if you carry out a process.

If your company does carry out design and development, but thinks it's relatively unimportant to the business or you would like to avoid this because you know this area is not a strong point in your business, you cannot just decide to exclude it. If your company carries out a function, you have no reasonable grounds for exclusion. You have a responsibility to your customers.

So as you can see, the scope is extremely important in evaluating your certification requirements and as a way of identifying your business for accreditation purposes.

18. Certification bodies

To accept the validity of a certificate, it is worth mentioning the role of third party accreditation and certification. This role is critical in giving consumer confidence that the rigours of assessment are applied. It also confirms that those supplying that assessment are themselves being assessed and passed for the role of being able to audit and give certificates where required.

This is the approach, which is almost always preferred in the UK, where a national overseeing body is applying standards to those providing certification services. That body is UKAS (United Kingdom Accreditation Service). UKAS is itself governed by the Department for Business Innovation and Skills (BIS). UKAS is overseen by HM Government, but it is a private sector body.

Accreditation bodies throughout the world exist with a similar arrangement; some examples of these are:

- JAS-ANZ is the government-appointed accreditation body for Australia and New Zealand.

- ANAB in United States of America, ANAB: ANSI-ASQ National Accreditation Board.

- RVA in the Netherlands, RVA: Raad Voor Accreditatie.

- IPAC: Portuguese Institute for Accreditation.

- JAB: Japan Accreditation Board.

Certification

My own personal recommendation of a certification body is WCS (World Certification Services) Limited based in Liverpool, they do operate worldwide however. http://www.world-cert.co.uk/

WCS is a family run organisation that pride themselves on professionalism, dedication to getting things right, hard work and customer driven focus, they are a shining example of how a certification body should behave and one that I wholly endorse for an approach if you are considering an international standard.

WCS are a very fair organisation, which prides itself on being there for the customer, nothing is too much trouble and they are guided by an exemplary businessman called Bill Slocombe. Bill is the operational director and a very professional character. They are rightly admired in the UK and are considered to be amongst the top echelon of service providers in this industry.

There are other major bodies, but I could not comment on them all and choose to reserve my praise for WCS because of their personal touch which I am familiar with.

Obviously, choosing a certification body is important. Some of the major ones to look out for in the UK are:

- WCS.
- BSI.
- Moody International.
- NQA.
- LRQA.
- Isoqar.

There are many more, but these are the ones that I sometimes work alongside or receive training from, or pass details so that my clients can receive a quote from them.

They are all worth approaching for assistance. Your choice may depend on your locality; some organisations want a certification body that is near to them or fairly local. Or size may be a factor; some organisations want to be accredited by larger organisations like BSI and BSI is also one of the best known.

If you choose one of these bodies, the auditors should be well qualified to come to your company. They are also examined through rigorous procedures that ensure that they are delivering the right service to you.

Check their websites out, give them a call and see which one is best for you and your organisation, and if anything takes your attention. It really is a matter of personal choice.

Before you choose a body to certify your organisation, it is wise to consider some of the following points.

- Is it accredited by a national or international body? The ones I have previously mentioned are all (at the time of writing) accredited by a national body, and some by more than one national body if they operate overseas as well.

- If it is not accredited nationally, is there a third-party accrediting body that certifies and monitors it?

- Does it have the scope to accredit you in your industry? (See section 19).

- Is it right for your budget?

- Does it charge expenses? (Some do, some don't)

- Do your customers recognise this body?

- Does it demonstrate care for your needs?

- Are its auditors available or do you have to book months in advance to get an audit date?

- What are its ongoing terms after certification?

- Are you tied in and does the organisation offer you any benefits from being with it?

Of course, certification is your choice, but choose wisely and pick the best option for your organisation. These bodies should provide an auditor with competence in the standard that you are applying and also competent in your sector.

Certification bodies have to ensure that their auditors measure up to their own guidelines and satisfy the accreditation body that they are using people of experience and the necessary technical qualifications in the sector in which they are applying certification purposes.

The amount of days for the certification body visit depends on the size of your organisation, how many sites there are and possibly on criteria stipulated to them by the national body.

Generally they will visit you once for an initial audit and then for the main audit this could be a few days or even more. The initial audit is (on average) one / two days because that is the stage where they assess your quality management system only and not the whole process. If you pass this without too many problems, it's on to stage two.

Visit the IAF (International Accreditation Forum) or UKAS (United Kingdom Accreditation Service) websites for further information.

19.   What is best for your organisation?

What is best for another organisation may not be suitable for you. It all depends on your needs and on whether the certification body can meet your demands.

The first step is to identify if the certification body can provide you with the scope of accreditation. As we have discussed previously, you should ensure that they are accredited for your area of business. If not, there are two possible outcomes:

1) The certification body may request that you allow them to be audited by a national accrediting body simultaneously as they audit your company for competence. In other words, they will be audited by an organisation like UKAS at the same time the certification body's auditors audit your organisation. (I must stress here that if this happens, an overseeing national body is inspecting them, not your organisation, UKAS/ANAB etc have to ensure that correct procedure is followed and that the correct experience is applied from the auditor and from the certification body's own processes.)

2) You simply look elsewhere. There are many bodies out there and someone somewhere will meet your requirements, so keep searching.

What you must never lose sight of is the fact that the people who carry out the auditing and certification function are *your* customers, not the other way around.

If you feel that you have been subjected to unnecessary auditing techniques or a biased audit, then you may have grounds to complain? People should always treat you fairly. The auditor should be highly professional; if you don't like the way yours behaves on audit, you can always request a different auditor next time around – and you don't need to specify the reason.

Sometimes auditors are questioned when their motives for raising issues are perfectly valid. This has happened to me: I've stopped an audit because of underperformance and I was complained about, so it happens. If you have a problem with an auditor, ensure that you have a valid reason for raising any issue with his or her boss. And be fair; it's a difficult role.

Auditors do a great job for these bodies. It's hard work and I know that they are under pressure to perform and pass an organisation. Inevitably, some organisations don't like the home truths that an auditor may convey as part of his or her professional report. Auditors (when not passing an organisation) should always be given the benefit of the doubt because some organisations do not deserve or justify their awards, until further information is sought.

Remember, ISO 9001 implementation isn't just about your paperwork and if you do your internal audits properly: it is about the whole organisation, how it works, what it does, how you apply your processes, whether you are doing what your customers want within legal constraints and contracts, and so on.

There are lots of matters to attend to; if you think that the auditor is going to come in and just look at your paperwork from a quality control perspective, you are in for a real surprise. On certification audits they are there to 'sample assess' the whole of your organisation (or to your scope); further down the line when they are doing their 'surveillance audits' they will look at some processes and not all. It is only when the certification audits and triennial audits come about that they will 'sample assess' each and every process that they have identified with you.

In the certification section I gave you some pointers of what to ask the body. We can now look at these questions in a bit more detail.

Is it accredited by a national or international body?
If it is, all well and good: they will be appropriately assessed by a reputable third party, and this will give you consumer confidence in your choice. If not, it may still be an excellent company and you may also want to ask some of the following questions.

Whether third-party accredited or not, you have to ask what product is right for you? In this world there is something for every organisation; you just have to make sure you get the right one for you. Only you can decide what is best for your company.

Does it have the scope to accredit you in your industry?

Will the body send an auditor who has knowledge of your sector? Do its people know what they are talking about? Do you want to see some credentials? If you request some background information I am sure that all bodies would be welcoming and helpful to you on this subject.

Is the body right for your budget?

This is an important question. Sometimes certification bodies will come and see you every six months, others once a year. They are guided by the national bodies and sometimes by what the auditor uncovers. If you perform well you may be put on 12-month visits, while less impressive performance (or the first few certification audits) may place you initially on 6-month visits.

You need to assess what the cost is at the start and budget for the costs you have been quoted before progressing. What are the charges for the initial visit and for the main certification visit? What other charges are there? You may be charged extra for each visit after certification? Check your quote thoroughly and make sure you know exactly what the charging structure is; if in doubt, ask.

If I request a quote on behalf of my clients and I do not understand something, I call them back and ask for further information. Never just assume the answer; you might end up with an unpleasant surprise when it is too late?

As I have said before, you are the customer. Never forget that. Ensure that you are happy with the cost before signing up. What you cannot do though is pay for one year and then not let them come back and see you. Certification usually comes with terms and conditions, and if you stop the audits and payments you will be asked to return your certificate or possibly face legal action?

Does it charge expenses?

Some certification bodies may claim expenses from you, and some won't. Ask them whether they charge, and if so, at what rate.

Do your customers recognise the body?

You may want to ask them. Are they asking you to have a certificate that is accredited by a third party? If so, is that third party a national body? Is it the one in the UK, or the one in the US, or wherever in the world?

If your customer is requesting that you implement any international or national standard and threatening to withdraw business if you don't, just ensure that they recognise the body that you are dealing with and its overseeing body. In the case of UKAS, ANAB etc, this should not really be an issue, but you never know. If you are a UK-based company and your customers are based in the USA they may ask you for ANAB accredited certificates. Conversely, if yours is a US-based company, your British customers may want UKAS accredited ones.

If you are unsure, ask. I'm currently assisting a multinational company and I put this question to them – which certainly made them assess what they really needed. The more information you can get on this subject from your customers, the better.

Does the body demonstrate care for your needs?

As I said before, the certification body is YOUR customer, so you should be treated promptly and professionally. Customer lines should be open and available, and you may even have access to a certification manager as well as an auditor. Some bodies like to have managers managing organisations in the certification process. I think this is a good idea.

Are its auditors available or do you have to book months in advance to get an audit date?

Some bodies have a shortage of good auditors; some are overstretched. Ask the body if it can provide certification in a timeframe that suits you – within reason. And give plenty of notice.

If you think that you'll need to speak to them in April, ring them in February. These bodies are busy and can have many thousands of customers to look after. When you contact them, be reasonable with your requests: although you want the best auditor for your business, if he or she is tied up for three months because there are others before you in the queue for certification, then you must be patient. My advice is to contact them earlier than you think you need to and go from there with reasonable requests.

What are its ongoing terms after certification?

As I mentioned previously, you may be tied in for a period of years (usually three). What does this all cost? What does this mean to your business? When are the visits to be scheduled and at what frequency? These are all questions that you need to keep in mind when approaching your selected proposals.

Are you tied in and does the organisation offer you any benefits from being with it?

The chances are that you may be tied in for a time, but check with the body. There will be 'get out' clauses but they may come with a cost?

The benefits of being with a certification body depend on how you and your customers view the certificate, and whether they recognise the certification body?

Other benefits may include providing you with a free certificate, a discount if you decide to be assessed against another standard with them, for example ISO 14001 or ISO 27001. The reason that they may be able to do this is that some systems are compatible with other systems; the documentation structure can be replicated and added to rather than completing a whole new system for each standard in a company. The ISO are aware of this and have helped with the amalgamation of standards as much as they can.

However, the main benefit is certification. Whichever body you choose to provide this service for you, you should be proud of yourselves in achieving the standards that you strive for.

20. What will the certification body look for in certification audits?

Everything! Certification bodies are there to ensure that your processes are working effectively. That means pretty much anything in your business (according to your agreed scope), and goes far further than simply checking quality documentation.

In my view, the quality management standard should be renamed a business management standard, because that's what it is. ISO 9001 encompasses all business practices in your organisation should you choose to have your whole business certificated, which most companies do these days.

A business that introduces the quality standard is implementing much more than a quality system; it is a system that is embedded into your business. The most effective way of incorporating it is to find out the areas you are weak on and introducing a few matters at a pace that suits you and your business, rather than introducing a whole new work ethic or work system that might alienate your employees. Find the gaps and fill them in.

The certification body will wish to sample your business and ensure that you conform to the requirements of the standard. When they come to see you, they have to look at samples because it just would not be feasible otherwise.

If you have 1000 quotes that year, the auditors may ask to look at five or six – unless of course mistakes start to be uncovered. If that happens, the auditor may dig a little deeper to find out if the issue is common or is just a one-off, and the way to do this is sample more records.

The auditors can ask to see anything in your business, within reason. If there are confidential matters then it is up to you to discuss them with the auditors and ensure that you have the correct legal assurances from them. Most audits nowadays start by informing you that everything that the auditors see is confidential between you, them, the certification body and maybe a national body if they themselves are audited.

The main task you should concentrate on as an implementer is to get the main departments together, discuss it with them and make sure you uncover dark areas that may constitute problems. ISO audit or not, most companies really know where most of their problems are. Hiding them will do you no good on audit – and you can bet that the auditor will find them!

If you have one hundred training records to choose from and you pick ten, I will put money on it that the auditor may find the one out of one hundred records that isn't filled in properly. In this case, I usually waive it if nine are okay, I would just make a note of it though as an observation. Or just tell them to do it straightaway, which usually does the trick.

The auditor should follow a logical sequence through your company. He or she will tell you at the start of the audit, or maybe inform you a week before, where s/he would like to go when they are with you. Although you can object, that will only raise suspicion and could lead to certification problems.

At the opening meeting you can discuss timeframes of where the auditor would like to be, so you can organise escorts. You cannot just let them wander alone.

At the start of your audit you should know exactly where you stand at any point. If the audits are going to last a few days, it's essential that you plan well and inform all who are involved.

When conducting an opening meeting or attending one, look at the human element of auditing and the perception of auditors. Following on from my remarks in previous sections, it is important that the auditor conveys a pleasant approach at this early stage; the last thing he or she wants to do is annoy you at the start!

The lead auditor should brief the management / directors to inform you all of how the audit may proceed throughout the organisation. The lead auditor would carry this out on a formal certification audit, or maybe even a supplier audit, if you carry these out. There will be representatives / auditors with them and the opening meeting will be attended by representatives of your organisation.

The opening meeting is usually carried out with the Management Representative (minimum) and should usually be accompanied by a director. It is sometimes useful to have audit guides or other managers present, but is important that a senior figure understands what is happening on audit.

The meeting will be chaired by the lead auditor and usually takes between 15 and 30 minutes depending on the size of your organisation. It will inform the attendees of how the audit is going to pan out throughout the day and who will be required at certain points. The plan of the audit will be given to the senior management and the quality representative and any issues shall be discussed at this point.

What will be discussed?

- Introduction and confidentiality.
- Scope of audit and exclusions if necessary.
- Availability of personnel and guides.
- Audit plan and locations.
- Use of a private room or area to confer.
- Raising of potential non-conformities.
- Health and safety points.
- Reporting issues, questions and further actions.
- Closing meeting time and location.

As an auditor, you need to ensure that your customers, auditees and guides know how you are planning to proceed.

Introductions are necessary if people do not know each other. It's common courtesy that everyone present knows everyone else. Also, remembering names is a great communication strategy and people are generally more responsive when addressed correctly. Sometimes a private office or room may be requested for the audit staff, depending on availability and location.

Confidentiality of the audit should be discussed. The auditees and your organisation should be at ease that what you discuss will not be aired with anyone apart from the audit team and the senior management. This is important, since lack of trust in this area can make auditees unwilling to divulge information.

Scope of the audit concerns what the boundaries of the audit are, how many standards are being audited against, what buildings or offices are concerned and whether there are any exclusions when auditing to ISO 9001.

Availability of personnel and guides is important on audit, as you will need access to people and areas. Ensuring that people are available at particular times is of paramount importance.

Audit plans and locations are to be discussed so that people are aware of where the auditor may be, who you are with and to ensure that available staff are in attendance. Audit plans show the auditee your aims and any rearrangements can be discussed.

Raising of potential non-conformities should be addressed to put people at ease to how that process works. Non-conformities are to be used as a tool for progress, not for bullying someone into action or 'telling tales' on people.

The raising of **health and safety** points is to be addressed so that you are aware of any potential dangers or concerns. Highlighting risks and dangerous areas should be included here, as well as fire safety precautions and evacuations. (Are there any practice alarms that day?)

Reporting issues, questions and further actions is to be conveyed to the organisation, auditees and team. This is to ensure a good dialogue occurs between the two parties. Any concerns or questions about the audit from your organisation should be addressed here.

The worst thing that can happen is that an auditor turns up at a business and you have not told certain people. That can really make the sparks fly! Make sure that you inform people one month, three weeks, two weeks and one week before the audit. On the day, it's also wise to have a look about the morning before the auditor turns up, make sure the place looks presentable and have pride in your workplace.

On a certification audit or supplier audit a **closing meeting** will be performed to highlight any issues or concerns – and also to mention any positive points, which is important. If there are problems early on in the audit, these should be conveyed at the time and there should be no surprises at the closing meeting.

Auditors' meetings / final meetings

Before the auditors discuss any findings with you, it will be important for them to compare notes and pool their conclusions. On certification audits, this should be done in a quiet office or room where they can have some privacy. This should be requested at the start of the audit so that any arrangements can be made easily. If an auditor is operating alone, a quiet and private room can also be beneficial.

The final meeting may discuss:

- The findings of the audit and various points.
- Group discussions and easing out of any complications between the parties.
- Discussions about non-conformance.
- Positive points (and a bit of back-slapping).
- What will be presented to the auditee / organisation?
- Conclusions and recommendations.

We do not always report every issue. It's important to get the nature of the audit across and to concentrate on any important issues to be resolved; auditing is a sample exercise.

Reporting to management

Once an audit has been completed and any non-conformances and observations noted, it is time to complete the report and discuss this with you and your directors and managers etc.

The whole purpose of a meeting is feedback: how has the audit progressed? The persons who should attend are the audit team, representatives of the company, quality manager, directors etc.

It is a not a minimum requirement, but at least two people should be present from your organisation, so that you can gather your thoughts and discuss this afterwards - and, out of respect for the auditor who has just spent a few days working hard to audit your company.

It is important that it is not just the quality representative attending: this can be highly stressful and awkward for the representative if he or she is on the receiving end of non-conformities. On certification audit, this meeting should be agreed upon at the opening meeting and there should be a room available for this if possible.

The format of this closing meeting may be the following:

- Thank you for allowing the audit to happen – it is good manners to include this at the start and can galvanise business relations between all parties.
- Confirmation of the scope, standard and objectives – informs you and your company what was the purpose of the audit, any exclusions and the objectives.
- Statement of confidentiality and informing of the sampling exercise – gives reassurance of the audit findings and explains the sample process to you.
- Who might view the audit record? – informs you and your organisation what happens if an accrediting national body looks at your file.

- Summary of the findings of the audit and the result – all-round positive feedback on the audit and explaining what was uncovered.

- Non-conformities and observations found during the audit – informs you about any problems or issues that may require rectifying. There should be no surprises (unless these were found late in the day).

- Discussions on the findings – feedback and discussions from the organisation. This will include whether you accept the findings.

- Appeals process – how to engage in the appeals process if required?

- Inform your organisation of recommendations – recommendations of future actions and timeframes if any immediate actions are needed.

- Explain any re-auditing / surveillance auditing processes in the future.

- Any further questions, and final thanks.

That should be it; if you are in any doubt as to what else should happen, get those auditors in to see you! There's no substitute for taking action.

Part 4: Do you need external professional assistance?

21. Consultants

Being a consultant in business and quality management can be quite tricky. Let's say I have ten clients at any one time, each revolving through the process until we get to the completion of their implementation or just general assistance with internal auditing. There are many processes in a business and many different people to interact with, many egos to smooth and directions to suggest so that I fulfil my customers' aims.

I know some extremely well qualified consultants; and they are some of the most highly skilled individuals I've met. That's not surprising. They have to get to know your process in a matter of months if not weeks, tuning themselves into your processes and then examining your needs. This takes practice and experience. Then they have to ensure that you are going to pass an international or national standard. That's a lot of pressure on the consultant.

The correct way for consultants to work with businesses, in my view, is to find out where the gaps are in your business, filling in those gaps and assisting you to get accreditation to whatever standard you are applying for.

This way, the customer is comfortable with the process, nothing is alien to them and it is all completed with the customer's authority and acceptance.

Consultants will generally find out what suits your business by a few experiments and through experience. They will then aim to ensure that any processes introduced are efficient, customer friendly and above all, workable to those who use them.

Most of us are there to guide, be a leader and co-manage a system until you are happy and satisfied that the system that you have helped to build alongside us is clear and working well.

Consultants should continue to support you until you are ready to accept the auditors in for certification, or at least until you are obviously on track to achieve your goal and are completely comfortable with your quality management system.

Which consultant should you choose? Only you can decide if a consultant is the right person for you. If you decide to appoint one, I recommend that you accept what they are saying and trust their professional judgement. But before that, let us explore some more points for you to consider.

I know quite a number of excellent consultants. I can't mention them all, but two in particular are of the highest class. These are Paul Plumridge of QuServe (www.qu-serve.co.uk) and Peter Bennett of BCS Quality (www.bcsquality.co.uk). Paul is in the Midlands and Peter is based in the North West of England. I learned some of my trade from them both in consultancy and auditing.

These two will come into your company, evaluate your business and help you to achieve your goal of a quality management system that is suitable to your needs, professional, workable and straightforward.

The other reason that I mention these two gentlemen is that they are also auditors on behalf of national bodies, so they know exactly what an auditor will be looking for when they come in.

Of course, they cannot audit you for the certificate as well. Auditors have to sign impartiality agreements and we cannot work with anybody in an auditing or consultancy role if we have worked with them on certification or consultancy in the past two to three years. In the world of third-party auditing, the auditor and consultant should be strictly independent of each other.

If you choose a consultant, it's best to get several in and ask a few questions, but to start with I would ask them a few questions on the telephone to find out which ones might suit you and those that definitely don't. After you've whittled down the number, you might want to get the likely ones into your offices to see how they look, dress and behave with you. If you ask a consultant to visit your offices, make sure that you have plenty to discuss.

What should you ask a consultant?

Here are some useful questions.

- What experience do they have in standards and implementing in your sector of business?

- What kind of service do they carry out? Is it bespoke or template driven?

- Does their consultancy have any tie-in over the months and years? Are there any retainers that you need to know about?

- Does the consultancy operate on a daily basis?

- Does the consultancy have any past clients that you can speak to for a reference?

- Does the consultant have any auditing experience? Although not always necessary, this certainly helps.

- Will they carry out your internal audits and management review for the fees quoted?

- Do they give you a breakdown of what they will be doing throughout the consultancy?

- Can you exit the agreement if you want to?

- Have they any past work to show you?

- Do they charge extra for expenses?

- Do they have a portfolio?

- How good are they at what they do? Ask them! Their answer will reveal a lot about them.

- Will they help you to choose a certification body?

- Will the system that they help to implement build on your present structure or be separate?

- If this system is separate, how does it work?

- How much do they cost?

- How long will they stay throughout the day to help you?

- Is the fee charged for all day or half a day, what are the hours they are staying with you?

- Are you expecting the consultant to do all of the work or are you going to assist him or her?

Remember: a consultant will never know your business as well as you do; so the more input you can provide, the better the service you'll get, and, it will probably cost you less.

It's important to treat consultants fairly. They deserve to be paid for the work they do just as anyone else does. Some people want you to start helping them for nothing: something I've encountered myself. After I have been in the first time, told them what they need and perhaps given them a few good pointers, I won't go back unless it is for paid consultancy.

I used to write all of my clients' procedures for them: now I ask my clients to do it themselves. It is better that someone writes a process that knows exactly what they are doing, and, if anything needs to be added a good consultant will certainly help you to add them.

In quality circles a consultant's role is very much hands-on. The best partnerships between clients and consultants are the ones in which the client accepts that the consultant is there to guide, not to do all of the work for you (although I am sure that many consultants will tell you that sometimes this is exactly what they have done). I have done it myself: I have dragged big companies through the hoops and got them to certification. That can be both difficult and frustrating.

In my earlier days some companies would put me in a room and expect me to just get on with it. I won't work that way now, for the simple reason that interaction between the two parties is absolutely paramount. I have gone in to some Managing Directors and said, "This is not working; you need to be a part of it or that's it."There's nothing worse than someone using you just to get a result. You have to be involved with each other.

You might be thinking that that's what you are paid to do. It is – but it's only part of it. A decent consultant is there to assist your business, help it to prosper, become more efficient and structured, not just to get you a tick on the wall. We are there to work with you and to bring value. Decent consultants want to help you, try new things, help you to explore your management role, assist you to become streamlined in certain areas, make you more professional.

Because of the nature of the work, getting to know each and everybody's business systems can be a daunting task – especially when you consider that some consultants may be assisting more than five or six businesses at a time. They may also be helping some clients with more than one standard. I can go all week without doing the same standard twice. And in any case, your consultant will be helping you on various parts of the business that need to come up to scratch, even if they're not requirements for ISO standards.

Okay, so we have explored using a consultant. What about not using one? In my opinion, this can be a false economy. If money is tight, consider using hiring a consultancy for just one day – which can save you twenty days of work. Prices are usually daily rate and range from £200 to over £1,000. Other places to help you find one are isostandardsconsultants.com.

If you choose not to use a consultant, cover yourself with other people's input; get other members of staff to read the ISO standard and ask them how they interpret it. The main issue you have on an implementation role is the understanding of the ISO 9001 standard if you do not have previous experience of it.

I am sometimes called up by people who know their businesses inside out. They're intelligent, hard working and efficient but simply don't understand the language that the ISO use. I can usually help them quickly and they are very happy.

People who have a 'can do' attitude tend to go far, having a good go at it on your own will give you a greater sense of fulfilment – and make you even prouder of yourself.

The best starting point is to write your main processes down and get people's input. Then look at the documentation requirements of the standard, complete them, do your audits, complete your management review and you're there...if only it were that easy.

If you use a consultant to help you, maybe you just want them to do your internal audits if money is tight in your business. I can understand this as a business owner myself. If you can only afford one or two days' assistance, get the auditor in at the start of your project to give you plenty of direction and then help you with the internal audits at the end before the certification body comes in. He or she will be able to help you to identify any potential weaknesses and then fix them.

If you go it alone, may I suggest using other standards to help you? ISO 19011 is a guideline for quality (and environmental) management systems auditing. This document can assist you to complete your internal audits.

ISO 9004 is a guideline for going a bit further than ISO 9001 and managing for sustained success. There are some excellent pointers in there too. The standards may retail at around £50 - £100, but can be worth it if you are going it alone. The ISO website can give you plenty of assistance.

I have asked many implementers if they have read ISO 9001 all of the way through. Some laugh, some say no. Some say yes – although I don't always believe them. And in any case, the only way to really grasp it is to read it three or four times at least

When I first started I had the good fortune of having a Managing Director / Chairman / boss / friend, Alan, who used to be a consultant and professional auditor in this sector, so he was an excellent mentor. Alan, a gentleman as ever, a perfect business role model and a man of high respect, was my 'go to' man. If I had a problem I could go to Alan so that he could explain it to me or unravel whatever was going through my mind, he could do the technical bit 'standing on his head' and the application part just as well, my training was from him.

I had the task of implementing ISO 9001 into two of his businesses. Because he was the owner of both of the companies, he had plenty of 'clout' which meant that I could get most things done smoothly. As I mentioned early in the book, if you get a director onside with this task, it can make this 100 per cent easier. Alan would give me plenty of support and he helped to set me firmly on the trail where I am now, so I would like to take this opportunity of thanking him very much. I wish you well Sir.

To get to the final result, whether or not you use a consultant, takes plenty of thought and hard work. Without someone's help, it's likely to be even harder.

Ask yourself, who your 'Alan and Bob' are in your organisation. In other words, who can assist you in this difficult role? Finding someone to help can make all the difference. Good luck!

22.   External certification and beyond

Well, here we are at the end of the book. Thanks for staying the course.

ISO 9001 is a great challenge for any organisation when implemented correctly. My advice is to embrace it with common sense and go for it without hesitation; many an organisation has started out small and with a decent business / quality system that has helped it to grow and maybe achieve international success.

So what happens after certification? Perhaps it is a route that encompasses other standards and systems?

What I always say to a client if they are wishing to take their management systems further is, what do you gain from that standard? Will it help to make you better, safer, healthier, more efficient? Will it give you better environmental management and prospects? Will it grow your profits? Will it keep your customers happy or help your business to become recognised? Will it add value in case you want to sell your company one day? Will it get you onto a tender list? Which is the favourite these days.

Whatever your reasons, you must always ask yourself these kinds of question. My main reasons to implement our standards are that it:

1. Makes my company safer

2. Make it more efficient

3. Adds value to it

4. Helps my staff to get the most out of themselves by giving them structure.

5. Adds value for tendering and quoting purposes

If you can identify with any of the questions and you are seriously considering putting your organisation through the process, then go for it. You can become more efficient, you can get ahead of your competitors – and above all you can be proud of a great achievement.

As we discussed earlier, standards are all around us: in our vehicles, in our homes and workplaces, in our airports and aircraft, in our electrical equipment and in our cookers, fridge freezers, X-boxes, play stations, laptops and desktops, servers, mobile telephones. They're in our trains, trams, taxis, television sets, radios, walkmans, ipods / ipads, software, hardware, baby clothes and toys. We see them in restaurants, food production, health and safety equipment, tools, garden furniture, power stations, gas, electric and water services, social services, police, fire, ambulance, search and rescue, lifeboats, mountain rescue, NASA, ship builders, oil rigs, teaching, Army, Royal Navy and the Royal Air Force... The list is nearly endless.

Just ask yourself one question: voluntary standards or not?

You wouldn't want to get in a train or aircraft or go to a restaurant that didn't have any standards, I'm sure. So why should your business be any different? Why should customers use your organisation if you don't have any standards? I think you'll agree that this is a fair question.

I wish you all the very best in your implementation task. Thank you for reading this book; it's my sincere hope that it helps you to succeed.

Contacts

http://bqmc.co.uk/

http://isostandardsconsultants.com

http://www.iso.org/iso/home.html

http://www.world-cert.co.uk/

http://www.moodyint.com/

http://www.qu-serve.co.uk/

http://www.bcsquality.co.uk/

http://www.atsite.co.uk/

http://www.bsigroup.com/